STUNT KITES II

NEW DESIGNS, BUGGIES AND BOATS

Text
  Servaas van der Horst and Nop Velthuizen
Photographs
  Jan Pit, Michèle Velthuizen-de Vries
Drawings
  Jan Pit

THOTH
PUBLISHERS

ACKNOWLEDGEMENTS

The authors wish to thank the following persons most warmly:
Peter van den Hamer, Cees van Hengel, Frans van der Horst Sr,
Jimmy Kniphorst, Arno van Leeuwen, Gerard van der Loo, Peter Lynn,
Peter Ruinard, Dominique Scholtes, Karin van der Straaten,
Michèle Velthuizen-de Vries and Richard Zandberg.

Servaas van der Horst & Nop Velthuizen

ISBN 90 6868 085 4 / NUGI 466

Photographs
    Jan Pit, Michèle Velthuizen-de Vries
    page 4 Wolf Beringer
    page 8r. Cory Roeseler
    page 38 r. Karin van der Straaten
    page 49 Henk Hilbrands
    page 88 Robert Scheers
Drawings
    Jan Pit
Cartoons
    Arno van Leeuwen

Translation
    Michèle Velthuizen-de Vries
Graphic Design
    Eric van den Berg, Utrecht
Printing
    Veenman Drukkers, Wageningen

Photo cover: The Piraña.

*Photo page 4: Wolf Beringer
steering his Parawing.
This UL 6 m² version can be
flown in light winds.*

Distribution in the USA by What's Up
4500 Chagrin River Road, Chagrin Falls, Ohio 44022, USA
Tel. 216-247-4222 Fax 216-247-4444

Distribution outside the USA (Kite Shops) by
Vlieger Op bv, Weteringkade 5a, 2515 AK Den Haag, the Netherlands
Tel. 70-3858586 Fax 70-3838541

Distribution outside the USA (Bookshops) by
THOTH Publishers, Prins Hendriklaan 13, 1404 AS Bussum, the Netherlands
Tel. 2159-44144 Fax 2159-43266

CONTENTS

INTRODUCTION

This book has been written with the experienced stunt kite flyer in mind. We therefore assume you possess a wide range of kites, control stunt kites faultlessly and are well acquainted with the workings of a sewing machine. And that you are ready for some new challenges.

Stunt Kites II is full of new challenges. There is something tricky about every kite described in this book: a bulge in the nose; a strip of gauze on the trailing edge; a complicated bridle.

We have treated buggy racing - sitting on a three-wheeled contraption and being pulled along the beach by a kite at 50 km/h - in detail. Want to go on the water? No problem. We provide the measurements for a catamaran that can be totally disassembled.

We explain how to make a profiled sail. We show you how to make a kite noiseless. We present the 'Dike Diaper', a clever invention to slow down team kites. We introduce eight new stunt kites, from the Ideal Learner's Kite - via the extremely manoeuvrable acrobatic stunter - to the first heavyweight quad-line stunter.

As far as we are concerned, the highlight of this book is the *Sputnik 4*, the most advanced stunt kite of its kind available today. Sparless, noiseless and virtually indestructible, Sputnik 4 is radically manoeuvrable and has a wide wind range as well as an alarming pull. We provide you with detailed construction plans for this superb kite.

Since we assume you are no longer a beginner you will not be spoon-fed in this book. Instead, more often than not we will make suggestions that are open to debate. Should you come up with a better solution to certain problems, we suggest you follow your own instinct.

FOREKNOWLEDGE

In writing this book we also assumed you have some knowledge of modern kite-construction materials such as: spinnaker nylon, Kevlar, Dacron, and carbon fibre tubing. You know how to reinforce Spectra lines and are capable of making your own steering grips.

In short, you are either well-acquainted with our first book (*Stunt Kites - To Make and Fly*) or you have accumulated knowledge through personal experience. Sometimes we will refer you to chapters and pages from our first book, but this does not mean you have to go out and buy it, nor is it a prerequisite for *Stunt Kites II*. The references are merely a reminder to those readers who already have *Stunt Kites - To Make and Fly*, or are familiar with it.

We have deliberately included a topic from our first book: Knots. From the many reactions received, we discovered that many readers found difficulty in understanding this subject. You will find a section on knots in Appendix VII.

1 SO, WHAT'S NEW?

Much has happened over the past few years. On summer days the beaches along the North Sea coast are studded with stunt kite flyers. Boats and buggies are being pulled at incredible speeds by cleverly designed manoeuvrable wings. Kite shops have mushroomed all over the world and the number of kite models available on the market today is close to 500. International team flying competitions are being held from the Gold Coast of Australia to the palm beaches of the Hawaiian islands. In the Netherlands more and more surf shops are switching over to stunt kites as surfing is gradually losing popularity and 'that thing on two lines' becomes commercially interesting.

A negative aspect of this new trend is also becoming increasingly apparent. Accidents have occurred in the US where kite flyers have been badly wounded. In the Netherlands a fatal accident has even occurred as a result of stunting. Stunt kite flying is now banned on several locations both in the Netherlands and in Germany, also as a result of sunbathers and strollers who found the noise intruding too much on the peace. 'Hot-cutting' spinnaker nylon has been deemed detrimental to health. Also, broken carbon and glass-fibre tubes are not recyclable and for years remain on rubbish dumps as non-degradable waste. The relationship between single line kite flyers and stunt kite flyers has deteriorated - single line fliers are now outnumbered and often find themselves having to leave the flying site after confrontations with stunt kite flyers.

And yet... another book on stunt kites? Yes. But we have given the above problems considerable thought and have decided to do something about them. We have made sure that the measurements of all the kites in this book are such that virtually not a single millimetre of synthetic fibre tubing will wind up in the rubbish bin. The design-it-yourself models range from low-noise to completely noiseless in order to minimise noise nuisance. We have even handled the subject of safety so exhaustively that you may think twice about setting foot on a beach again.

Stunt kite flying has become considerably easier over the last few years. This is most apparent when launching a kite. The perpetual clumsiness associated with getting a Dykehopper or a Speedwing airbourne is over. The magic word? Camber.
In all other fields of non-powered aviation (hang-gliding, paragliding, parasailing, sky diving, gliding, etc.) our colleagues have long understood that a flat surface does not function very well as a lifting device. The lift per square metre of a flat surface is much less than that of a wing profile, and the angle of incidence of a flat surface is also much more critical.

For this reason, the first profiled kites which appeared some 15 years ago were revolutionary in terms of speed and pull; the Flexifoil still being the fastest commercial kite in existence. Obviously the challenge for us was to combine the characteristics of such a flying wing with a conventional flat stunt kite. We managed to do this by experimenting with countless variations of the Speedwing and, as a result, we noticed that by simply adding some fabric to the kite's nose so that it would billow, the stunter became much easier to launch, it pulled harder and it became completely silent.

The next development: the gauze strip. Sometimes a flyer doesn't want the kite to pull harder at all but wants it to become still. This is especially true in team flying where traction can be an inconvenience. So then out goes the camber and in comes the gauze strip. As a result the kite becomes noiseless without affecting its performance. The gauze strip replaces the last centimetres of the kite's trailing edge - where incidentally the noise originates - and prevents this from flapping, which is disastrous for the airflow around the sail.

In some cases the solution to the noise problem is even simpler. A string through the hem of the trailing edge will make almost any kite soundless. The operation is done in a few minutes and by varying the tension on the line the optimum adjustment can quickly be determined. Readers who understand advanced aerodynamics may be horrified by this solution: all you are doing is letting the trailing edge scoop up air. In other words, you are providing the kite with a built-in brake system. In reality, though, the loss of speed is not very noticeable and all of a sudden the beach is pleasantly quiet again.

The most noticeable development in the stunt kite world in recent years has been so-called 'power-kiting' in which the kite functions as a traction device. If you have ever felt the pull of a Speedwing in a storm, for example, you will realise that this force might serve some purpose.

In its simplest form the energy from such a kite can be used to drag you down wind. A packed lunch in your backpack, a harness around your hips, a sturdy control rod in your hands, gym shoes or skis on your feet and off you go speeding towards the horizon. Ten kilometres further on you take the bus back and start all over again. It will be obvious that we are not too excited about this method.

So let us take a look at our neighbours, the wind surfers on wheels. These surfers stand on a narrow board with four wheels and hold onto the boom of the sail. Their speed is impressive and - like a sailing boat - they can sail into the wind ('upwind'), having the advantage of being able to return to their

1 *Quad-line Bat by Uwe Gryzbeck.*

2 *Tandem-buggying along the beach. High speeds after slow acceleration.*

3 *Body-surfing.*

starting point. But a surf board is useless for a kite flyer - the kite will immediately pull the flyer off the board.

So what about roller skates? The American Lee Sedgewick uses a sparless quad-line stunter and wears a pair of skeelers (roller skates with four or five lined-up wheels). It seems to work. But even after you have put on protective clothing and look like a balloon, it still hurts every time you fall. No, there has to be a better alternative.

Peter Lynn from Ashburton, New Zealand, found one. Since 1991 Lynn has been producing a stainless steel contraption on three wheels called the buggy. The kite flyer sits between the two rear wheels a few centimetres above the ground and controls the front wheel with the feet. In this way, the hands are free to control the kite. A buggy rider launches his/her kite, steps

4 Whistling past other skaters: ice-buggying effortlessly across a frozen lake in Holland.

5 Potentially the fastest sailing device in the world: water-skiing behind kites.

into the cart, places the feet on the steering bars and brings the kite to the centre of the wind power zone. The buggy rushes forward, the pilot steers the buggy into a reaching course (cross wind) while dipping the kite in and out of the wind power zone and before you know it the speedometer is nudging 90 kilometres an hour.

At the end of the stretch the kite flyer places the kite directly behind him/her, throws the body sideways and - like a skid course - makes a 180 degree turn. The rear wheels come to a halt, sand piles up a metre high and a second later the buggy is back on course with the kite back in position and the pilot heading again for the starting point. We have averaged speeds of more than 40 km/h during roundtrips on 15 km stretches of beach.

Is the beach too crowded or do you need cooling off? Then head for the open sea. After building and trying out some 60 prototypes, Lynn finally came up with a reasonably satisfactory three-hulled boat. The trimaran consists of three hulls of equal length (approx. 2 metres), in total barely weighing 20 kilos. The central hull is situated ahead of the two outer ones. The procedure is similar to buggying: position the kite above your head, step in, bring the kite into the wind power zone and take off. Highest speed: 20 knots.

The main snag with 'kite-sailing' is that the kite can drop into the water should the lines slacken. In a buggy you can prevent this by steering the buggy into the wind ('up wind'), but the trimaran is much too slow for such a man-

NEW!

The latest buggy-boat by Peter Lynn - the Kite Surfer - has revolutionised kite-sailing. Lynn got his inspiration for the unusual shape of the hulls from the world's fastest sailing boat, the Yellow Pages. The hulls have just enough buoyancy to prevent the navigator and boat from sinking, but as soon as the Surfer gains momentum the hulls start planing, making extremely high speeds possible. The Surfer is also fairly easy to steer.

Because the Kite Surfer has only been on the market since May 1994, no record-attempts have been made; it is therefore difficult to assess the maximum speeds of this boat.

The Kite Surfer weighs 15 kg and can be assembled within 20 minutes. Folded up, the boat can easily be stashed away in a large weekend bag. An international patent is pending.

oeuvre. Another problem is speed. Twenty knots (35 km/h) is wonderful for a boat of this length but it does not even come close to the sailboat's world record (*Yellow Pages*, 1993, 85.5 km/h) nor to the world's fastest surf board (Thierry Bielak, 1993, 83.96 km/h). And as long as speed and user-friendliness are inferior to the more conventional sailing crafts, kite-sailing will no doubt remain something of a fun sport for truly fanatical stunt kite flyers.

Any developments in the field of quad-line kites? Yes, but nothing particularly spectacular. In America the Quadrifoil, a sparless wing with two extra lines on its trailing edge, has made its debut. The kite resembles a modern manoeuvrable parachute and comes in all sizes. What is noteworthy of the Quadrifoil is that in strong winds even the smallest model has a significant pull.

Fortunately, from an artistic viewpoint there have been new developments in quad-line kite designs. Graceful peace-dove and bat-shaped kites have appeared, flying extremely well. In this book we introduce the long-snouted elephant - the Quadriphant - and we are convinced that in future the shapes of quad-line kites will become even wilder. Will you be the next designer?

And finally, Sputnik 4, the Dutch cousin of the Peel - also an invention of Peter Lynn. But there is so much to be said about sparless kites that we have covered it in a chapter all of its own. Well then, shall we begin?

2 ACCIDENTS AND NOISE

Let us start with the accidents first. We are on a beach with 50 km/h winds from the sea. A heavy-set man with a beard is about to launch a large version of the *Vector*, a sturdy TOTL *Hawaiian*-type kite. The man readies the kite while his wife - smaller, lighter and quite adept at flying a *Peter Powell* - takes the grips. The man throws the kite up. After a few hesitating moments the kite finds its bearings and all of a sudden shoots up with a roar into the direction of the stratosphere. The woman is thrust forward, lands on her stomach and gets dragged along the beach for quite a distance before she finally releases the grips. The kite comes crashing down, missing a woman sitting on the beach by a few centimetres. The man - believe it or not - first inspects his kite and only then checks to see whether his wife is alright or not.

Forgive the cliché, but Europe is a densely populated continent. Beaches along the coastline are used intensively by bathers - especially during the summer months - so obviously kite flyers should adopt an attitude of discretion when flying stunt kites. But apart from consideration for others, there is, more importantly, the safety factor. One only has to look around to see how many small mistakes can easily turn into scenes of horror. Let us take a look at some real-life examples.

The beach is as smooth and hard as a billiard table. With consistent, strong

winds from behind, a lone buggy rider races by at 60 km/h. But whoops, he does not see the pothole ahead and in a single 'graceful' movement he is flung out of his buggy. Without its driver, the buggy continues on its course down the beach, its speed hardly decreasing. Some kids playing do not see the buggy heading their way but fortunately it misses them by a few centimetres.

A boy has a whopper of a kite called the *Widowmaker* (whoever thought of this kite's name must be some misanthropist!). The boy lends his kite to his 14-year-old friend who has never flown a kite before. Tempting fate, the boy persuades his friend to wear a harness as well. Once again, on a beach, 5 Beaufort winds. The Widowmaker takes off like a rocket, the flyer finds himself catapulting forward and, after a few uncontrollable wild jumps, ends up landing head-first onto a basalt block next to the boulevard. Result: severe brain-concussion.

The island of Vlieland in the Netherlands and light steady winds. A very experienced buggy rider is frustrated with the slack winds and decides to launch the largest kite he has (7.5 m²). He plans to buggy the full length of the island (32 km), so he puts on a harness to relieve himself of some of the pull. He grins and thinks of the fun he is going to have. As he takes off, the pull of the kite increases and so does his speed: the rider begins to have second thoughts about his adventure. But before he can change plans there is a sudden strong gust of wind; although the experienced rider does everything he should do in such a situation - including bringing the kite above his head in order to decrease the pull - it is to no avail. He is lifted right out of his buggy and ends up precariously hanging several meters above his buggy which continues at a good speed along its course. Finally the wind slackens and the rider is gently returned to earth. He was lucky, this time.

Den Helder, again in the Netherlands, and strong offshore winds. A kite flyer puts on a harness, attaches a sturdy kite to it and launches the kite. In offshore winds! Within a few seconds the flyer finds himself struggling with the kite which eventually drags him into the sea. Panic breaks out on the beach among the onlookers and a rescue team is quickly sent out after him. Fortunately the flyer has the sense to use his quick-release system (so that the line disconnects itself from the grips) and the flyer manages to swim back to the safety of the beach. The rescue team saves the kite instead. The incident makes next day's headlines.

What we are trying to say here is that a harness is often the cause of unsafe flying. The problem with a harness is that in times of danger - just when panic seems imminent - a flyer must make a resolute attempt to release himself (sometimes with pure muscle power) from his kite. Fortunately, there are safety-release grips on the market: by simply releasing the grips, the lines detach themselves from the grips and the kite flutters away. If not equipped with a quick-release system,

1 Peter Lynn safety-release handles; the control lines detach themselves from the handles when released.

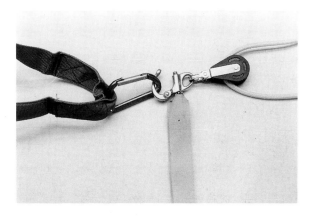

2 The 'quick-release' or 'safety-release' shackle: not quick and not safe.

grips and control bars can become dangerous projectiles when released in emergencies - they can harm people, animals and objects as they fly through the air.

The moral of all this? Stunt kite flying is an activity where anything that can go wrong, often does. Kites can, in the most ridiculous and unexpected situations, cause harm both to you and to others. So always use your head - always assume that there is the chance of something going wrong. If you think a stunt is dangerous, do not do it. If, for some reason, you do cause an accident, you had better be well insured. Standard third party liability insurances in the Netherlands only cover kites up to *one and a half square metres.* This applies to *all* insurance companies. So you basically have three choices: fly small kites only, continue flying kites without an insurance and risk possible bankruptcy, or get a supplementary third party liability insurance. You can also contact your local kite club or association: they should be able to give you advice concerning insurance; they sometimes even offer third party liability insurances to their own members. In any case, if you are involved in power-kiting there is a very real chance that you will injure yourself, so you should at least have a good medical insurance.

And finally, noise pollution. Some kite flyers enjoy sharing their demonic artistry with the entire neighbourhood, deliberately flying their kites right over the heads of innocent bystanders and preferable flying the noisiest kites available. As a result, strollers are becoming more and more nervous. If stunt kite flying ever becomes prohibited in the Netherlands it will be mainly because of such selfish, brainless, and childish behaviour. Do not spoil the fun for everyone just because you have the urge to show off - there are other ways to get the undi-vided attention of the opposite sex (see chapter on 'Aerobatics'). In the chapter 'The Camber' you will also find some of the techniques you can use to reduce the noise of your kite.

SURVIVING STUNT KITE FLYING

1 Do not fly in the vicinity of overhead electric cables, tram and railroad lines and roads.
2 Only use a harness when you have total control of the kite.
3 Do not fly your kite above bystanders.
4 Fly kites that are almost or completely soundless.
5 Only fly those kites you can control completely. Flying a 5 m² kite in 6 Beaufort winds is asking for trouble.
6 Do not jump or lift with your kites. You not only risk injuring yourself (this has happened many times) - worse, you risk killing yourself (this has happened too).
7 Do not use Kevlar control lines. Kevlar cuts other lines and can cause painful burn marks.
8 Talk to the other flyers on the flying site so that you do not get in each other's way. Stay away from single-line flyers - they are not as mobile as you are.
9 Get a supplementary third party liability insurance and make sure it covers all aspects of kite flying (buggying, power-kiting etc.), regardless of the kite's surface area.
10 Do not fly stunt kites in crowded kite festivals. If you must, then use a sparless kite; these have the least amount of impact in case of a crash or other mishap.

3 NEW MATERIALS

1 *A spinnaker weaving-machine in the Carrington factory.*

2 *Carbon fibre tubes. From top to bottom: thick-walled, standard and thin-walled. Notice the (white) glassfibre in the thick-walled tube.*

At first glance, nothing much has changed. Carbon fibre tubes are still black, Kevlar is still yellow and spinnaker nylon comes in all the colours of the rainbow. But if you take a closer look, you will notice that all the high-tech material has become even more high-tech. Everything is lighter, more rigid, ultraviolet-resistant and...more expensive. Let's start with carbon fibre.

CARBON FIBRE

A tube made out of carbon fibre is not rigid because carbon fibres are so rigid. On the contrary, fibres consisting of pure carbon are in fact completely slack, like sewing thread. The strength of carbon fibre lies in the fact that the material has a very low elasticity .

If you bend a carbon fibre tube, the fibres on the inside of the bend will compress while those on the outside must stretch. Carbon fibre resists this - the reason why carbon fibre tubes feel so rigid. There are various types of carbon fibre, some stretching less than others, indicated by the so called 'Modulus of Elasticity'. Low-Modulus carbon fibre has a higher stretch and is strong while High-Modulus carbon fibre has an extremely low stretch but is brittle.

The fibres are soaked in a resin (polyester-epoxy etc.) which, after harden-

ing, keeps them in place. A carbon fibre tube without resin is completely soft and a resin tube without carbon fibre is terribly brittle. Combine the two, however, and you have the lightest and strongest tube.

Two methods are used to produce carbon fibre tubes: pultrusion and wrapping. Pultrusion is a technique similar to that of extrusion where material is pressed through a hole (much like toothpaste being pushed through the nozzle of its tube), the form of which determines the shape of the final product. In the case of pultrusion, however, the product is extracted from the hole rather than pushed through it, so that fibres can be added in the process.

The following explanation deals with pultruded tubes with an 8 mm outer diameter and a 6 mm inner one.

A 30 m long machine is used for this process, equipped with a 1.5 m long stainless steel tube - the outer mould - at the front. The mould, in this case, has a diameter of 8 mm. A stainless steel rod with a 6 mm outer diameter is suspended exactly in the centre of the outer mould. This rod is held in place by a frame located in front of the mould. The positioning of this rod is extremely precise work. For example, if the rod were to shift or bend away from the centre of the outer mould, due to its weight, for example, the walls of the tubes

would end up differing in thickness - one side thick, the other side thin - and breakage would be inevitable. The French manufacturer Beman placed its machine vertically so that the central rod hangs straight down, thus solving the gravity problem.

The bundles of carbon fibre ('roving'), wound on enormous spools, are fed through a gap between the holder and the outer mould. Usually between 20 and 40 bundles of fibre are used to make one tube. The fibre bundles are continuously guided from the spool into a resin bath and then disappear into the front of the mould via the split between the central rod and the outer mould. You have probably guessed that the split is 1 mm wide all the way around.

On the other end of the metal mould, a double-caterpillar track pulls out the fibres and the resin strongly but slowly. This is what gives the process its name.

The stainless steel outer mould is heated to a precise temperature. As the fibre-bundles travel through the outer mould at roughly 1 cm per second, the resin hardens as a result of the heat. What goes in as a cluster of limp fibres soaked in resin comes out a metre and a half further on as a hard, rigid tube. A tube produced in this way is very rigid and light, but also vulnerable due to the fibres being merely held together by resin, which is not very strong. If a kite with such tubes were to crash to the ground, the tubes would most likely split from top to bottom. Most manufacturers, therefore, add an in-between layer with a different fibre-orientation (e.g. crisscrossed instead of straight) so that the tube is more split-resistant and, as a kite-frame, more crash-resistant. The metrical tubes of the Finnish company Exel are produced with an in-between fleece of glass-fibre. Other manufacturers use a winding technique - either 'spiral-winding' or 'cross-winding' on the surface or inside the tubes.

The technique of pultrusion has many advantages. Firstly, it is a continuous process so the tubes can be made to any length (even kilometres). Secondly, the machine can produce several tubes at once as several tubes come out parallel to each other. In this way costs are reduced considerably. Thirdly, the process is entirely automated. With no human worker overseeing the process, the pultrusion machine squeezes out 1 cm per second, 36 metres per hour, 864 metres per day, 315,360 metres per year.

The wrapping process works quite differently. There is no outer mould, only a central mandrel which is usually no longer than a metre. A strip of resin-impregnated carbon fibre webbing ('pre-preg') is wound either mechanically or

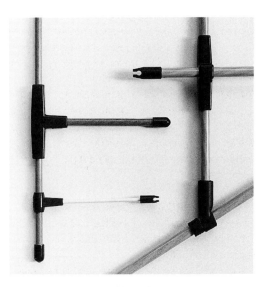

3 Nylon cross-joints and flexible connectors.

by hand around the mandrel. The quantity of pre-preg determines the rigidity and weight of the tube. Then tape is wound around the entire tube to keep it compact. The mandrel + pre-preg + tape is then placed in an oven, the resin hardens and finally the mandrel is removed from the centre of the tube.

The winding process has advantages too. By using this technique, extremely thin-walled tubes can be produced. The manufacturer can also produce tubes according to the wishes of clients - winding many or a few layers, inbetween layers of different material, thicker or reinforced tube-ends etc.

But this process also has disadvantages. The tubes can never be longer than the mandrel, which usually means no more than a metre. A longer mandrel will most certainly bend, resulting in crooked tubes.

It is difficult to make tubes completely regular. It is also economically disadvantageous: the machine can only produce one tube at a time. Wrapped tubes are therefore more expensive than pultruded tubes.

Your local kite store may also sell Ultra-light tubes. These tubes are much lighter, have a thinner wall and yet are very rigid. The manufacturers accomplish this by using carbon fibre with a higher E-Modulus, which means that this carbon fibre shows less stretch. One noticeable disadvantage: this 'improved' carbon fibre tube is also more brittle. In other words, Ultra-light tubes weigh less and feel just as rigid, if not more rigid, but break easier and cost extra. These tubes are for those who prefer to fly in light winds.

There is also a new series of thick-walled pultruded tubes on the market. These were invented so that the tubes retain the same diameter but are stronger. This was done by adding carbon fibre or glass-fibre to the inside of the tubes. Among the thick-walled tubes, some are now 20 per cent thicker and heavier, have about the same rigidity, but...they are 100 per cent more break-resistant!

SPINNAKER

Since 1993, every kite maker has had to make the difficult decision of whether to use spinnaker *nylon* or spinnaker *polyester*, both superb fabrics in their own right.

Spinnaker polyester is 25 per cent lighter than nylon, totally air-tight, does not absorb water (nylon swells 2.2 per cent and is heavier when wet) and its colours fade four times slower than nylon in sunlight. Its stretch - both lengthwise and on the bias - is also considerably less than nylon.

But there are two major disadvantages to polyester: it is less rip-resistant (if a rip appears in the fabric, the chance that it will eventually rip completely is greater), and it is expensive. Spinnaker polyester usually costs about 60 per cent more than spinnaker nylon.

These polyester properties are especially noticeable in large sparless kites flown in light winds.

At the moment, there is only one brand of polyester fabric on the market: Icarex. It is produced in Japan and comes in three grades: P 31, weighing 35 grams per square metre; P 38, weighing 42 grams; and PL 62, weighing 65 grams, which is coated with a layer of mylar-monofilm.

Even if you decide to use nylon, you still have a problem selecting the fabric. Besides 'conventional' spinnaker nylon, there is also *High Tenacity* nylon, a greater rip-resistant fabric. Its price is also higher than that of standard spinnaker nylon. It is not always easy to distinguish the numerous types of nylon stocked by your local kite store, but here is what you can do to test the fabric: pinch the material between the nails of your thumb and fore-finger and try ripping it. If it rips without you having to make a notch first,

then it is not High-Tenacity fabric. There is also the choice of fabric with silicone-coating or polyurethane coating. Silicone-coated fabric is incredibly rip-resistant but almost impossible to work with; it literally slithers away from your cutting-table and sewing machine.

Finally, there is a difference between fabric that has had little calandering and fabric that has had a lot. The former is soft, tear-resistant and elastic; the latter feels more like paper - rigid, easy to tear and with little stretch (Cf. *Stunt Kites - To Make and Fly*, page 49).

To put it simply, the success of your kite depends largely on the type of material you wind up choosing. In other words, feel the various fabrics in the shops with your hands (blow and suck on them if you have to), talk to the shop assistants (and tear the material when they are not looking), raid their technical brochures, reconsider your options for a few hours and then buy your 30 cm of spinnaker fabric!

LINE

Dyneema/Spectra line is still the strongest and lightest line available. In the last few years DSM, the inventor of Dyneema, has succeeded in strengthening polyethylene fibre by 20 per cent. DSM now also produces 200 denier fibres - i.e. the strands weigh 200 grams per 9,000 metres. Until recently they used 400 denier. By weaving more of these thin strands (now it is 16 - it used to be 8 for the 75 kg line) a smoother, thinner and lighter line is produced.

Shanti in the US has come up with the so-called Zip-line, a mixture of Spectra and Dacron strands. The Zip-line is much thicker and heavier than a 100 per cent Spectra line of similar breaking strength and is therefore not meant for optimum performance. But because the line contains Dacron, it is much easier to knot. Dacron acts as a sort of 'built-in cushion', making the sleeves on the ends of the line superfluous. The advantage of Zip-line is that, like Spectra, it hardly stretches.

Zip-line is a good alternative to Skybond and Dynacore, both of which consist of low-stretch material (Kevlar and Dyneema, respectively) in the centre and a polyester sleeve. In reality, however, this combination creates problems. Due to the huge difference in stretch, the sleeves and central material do not complement each other that well and before long one or the other snaps or becomes damaged. This is not the case with Zip-line.

4 THE WORKING AREA

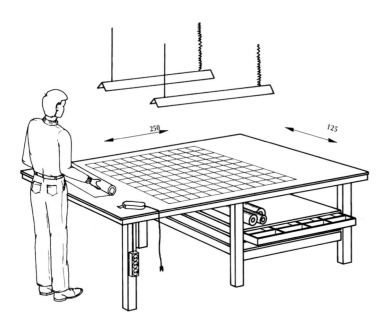

So you have decided to take kite-making more seriously. The first thing you need to consider is your working-table. An average kitchen table is 80 cm wide, 120 cm long and 76 cm high - fine for a small Speedwing, a bit difficult for a Spin-off and virtually impossible for a large Sputnik.

Your local timber yard should be able to solve your problem. Chipboard, or better yet, MDF board is what you need. These boards are usually 125 cm wide and 250 cm long. A perfect size for your needs. But now you must ask yourself, "Where on earth do I put it?" If you paint one side of the board green, turning it over will produce a ping pong table, perhaps a simple compromise to win over your family.

MDF boards come in various thicknesses. Do not select a board less than 12 mm thick or you may end up with a warped table. The height of the table depends on your own height. You should make it high enough to work comfortably while standing up, since you will find yourself doing most of the work in that position. You can measure the proper height by stretching out your arms from the elbows at a perpendicular angle to your body; lower them slightly and measure the distance between the palms of your hands and the floor.

Because the table will be considerably higher than an average kitchen one, you will have plenty of room underneath. This is a great place to stash away templates (before you know it you will have quite a pile), carbon and glass-fibre rods and small tools. Even an old type-case will become useful again: place it on its back and use it as a drawer under your table (an L-frame on either side will keep it in place) for all sorts of small items such as rings and connectors. You can also attach a multiple plug socket onto one of the legs of the table to operate your sewing machine, soldering iron etc. Place the table in such a way that you can at least stand at one of the long and one of the short sides of it.

The table is finished off with a few coats of white paint (lightly sandpapered between coatings), then with a marker draw a latticed pattern of 10 cm squares onto the table. Having done this, add a few coatings of transparent varnish over the whole table.

The second most important item in the workshop is lighting. Fluorescent tubes are probably the best for this. Place at least two tubes above the table, spaced evenly apart, about 70 cm above the surface of the table (placing the tubes lower will certainly give more light, but the tubes will also become more vulnerable to swaying arms and rods). Use 36 Watt tubes, about 120 cm long, of the cool white (working-light) kind.

A few remarks about the soldering iron. On the one hand, we recommend you replace your soldering iron with a so-called 'hot-knife'. This device is used by sail manufacturers, resembles a soldering-pistol, heats up within 8 seconds (600 degrees Celsius - so you can melt off the ends of bridle lines quickly) and uses far less energy than a conventional soldering iron. However, it is also pricey: about US$ 100. On the other hand, as research on the part of the German *Drachenmagazin* shows, hot-cutting spinnaker nylon may be detrimental to your health. Despite their diligent detective work, however, the Germans have yet to discover just what toxic chemicals spinnaker nylon consists of. Yet another mystery is the type (and amount) of toxic chemicals released when hot-cutting spinnaker nylon. What the researchers strongly advise though is that you hot-cut spinnaker nylon in a well ventilated area. Having experienced lightheadedness on a number of occasions after hot-cutting spinnaker, we have come to the same conclusion. We therefore recommend the use of scissors and cutters instead of a hot-cutter whenever possible.

'Cold-cutting' works best with a Stanley snap-off blade knife, the only knife

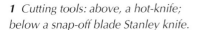

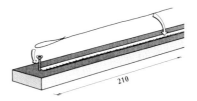

3 *A bridle-plank: creates accurate bridle lines.*

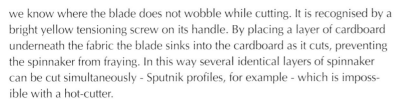

1 *Cutting tools: above, a hot-knife; below a snap-off blade Stanley knife.*

2 *The transporter of a Pfaff (in the photograph, left, next to the press-foot) which makes a rake-like movement similar to the lower transporter.*

we know where the blade does not wobble while cutting. It is recognised by a bright yellow tensioning screw on its handle. By placing a layer of cardboard underneath the fabric the blade sinks into the cardboard as it cuts, preventing the spinnaker from fraying. In this way several identical layers of spinnaker can be cut simultaneously - Sputnik profiles, for example - which is impossible with a hot-cutter.

The next thing to improve in your working area is the sewing machine. Ninety percent of all sewing can be accomplished on a conventional home sewing machine. In some cases (when sewing heavily reinforced nose pieces, e.g.) an industrial machine does come in handy. The most expensive machines (brand names such as Yuki and Pfaff) have impressive motors which can be suspended under the working-table for a flat and spacious work surface. Moreover, these machines are equipped with so-called needle transports - a truly clever invention. Not only do these sewing machines pull the fabric with a transporter (moving teeth which appear through the foot plate), but the needle itself functions as a sort of rake, preventing the upper layer of fabric from sliding away from the bottom layer. The only problem with these machines is their noise and high price. Even second-hand, these superb machines cost more than US$ 500 and most of them cannot even sew zig-zag. A good alternative is the so-called semi-industrial sewing machine; a heavy, reliable machine but with a lighter motor that can also be built into the working-table.

Pfaff has sewing machines on the market with a press-foot consisting of two transporters. The upper transporter moves with the lower transporter and

together they function like a pair of pliers so that the fabric cannot slide away. This system is ideal for making kites. In fact, slippery fabric can be transported in this way as easily as with a needle-transporter type industrial machine, while zig-zag stitching is also possible. Other brands of sewing machines again offer similar accessories.

As to the measuring tools, you will soon find triangle and conventional rulers inadequate. The best alternative is a long flat strip of aluminum, about 1 to 1.5 m in length, available in art supply shops. These aluminum rulers are equipped with rubber on the bottom to keep the ruler from slipping on the fabric, a metal edge for cutting and an accurate centimetre scale.

Unfortunately these are also quite expensive. But there is a simple and cheap alternative: purchase a flat strip of aluminum (40 x 4 mm) from your local hardware store. Pick a completely straight strip of aluminum and have it cut to a length of 1.1 to 1.6 m, that is to say, to a length which is longer than the width of the most common fabric available. Mark the ruler as accurately as possible or glue an old measuring tape onto it. To keep the ruler from sliding, glue a strip of rubber onto the bottom.

Sometimes it will be necessary to measure large triangles with a compass (e.g. when making a Speedwing). This can be done with a piece of line and a pencil, but there is a smarter way to accomplish this. Some brands of measuring tapes (Fisko) have a built-in compass which is extremely accurate.

To mark large perpendicular angles use a sheet of cardboard. Most cardboard sheets are 80 x 100 cm and have four perfect perpendicular angles.

If you want to create an even more professional workshop, you can always add a drill column, a lathe, a spinnaker-roller, a computer plotter, a welder and...dozens of other useful machines. By then you will be within easy reach of a Technical College degree!

5 THE CAMBER

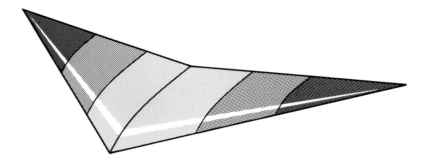

1 Speedwing with parallel camber seams...

We tried a simple experiment. We put together a standard Speedwing with a flat sail and a Speedwing Super with an extra sail-billow near the nose and set the two kites up alongside one another on the beach. Using lines of equal length and breaking strength, we flew the kites in steady, 4 Beaufort winds from the sea.

And guess what? The Speedwing Super was easier to launch, made less noise and pulled harder and more consistently than the standard Speedwing. Even at the edge of the window the pull was considerable. Conclusion: Speedwings with a billowed nose are better than conventional Speedwings.

The curvature in the sail of such a kite is due to excess fabric in the nose. The wind pushes this fabric outwards, whereby the nose billows and all of a sudden the kite has a wing profile.

Kites with wing profiles create much more lift than kites of similar size but with flat surfaces. The air particles at the top of the profile (the billowing part) are forced to make a detour, causing the air particles to flow faster in order to join those at the bottom of the profile flowing in a straight line. Because the detouring air particles at the top flow faster, they have less time to exert pressure on the kite sail, thus creating a low pressure area, i.e. suction. The theory is that two thirds of total lift is created by suction. The other third is caused by wind pressure on the bottom side of the profile: high pressure. Most of the lift (about 80 per cent) generated by suction (on the top side) occurs at 10 per cent of the front of the profile, by the leading edge of the kite, that is. This is why the leading edge is considered such an important part of the kite.

A deep billow at the leading edge is also important because of its greater tolerance for changes in the angle of attack. According to Marchaj (Cf. Reading List), sails with a deep curvature have a better lift over a wider range of angle of incidence than flat surfaces. In flying stunt kites this implies that bridle adjustments for kites with deeply billowed sails are less critical. For the same reason they are much harder to stall.

It is a simple thing to demonstrate how billowing works. If you sew together two pieces of fabric the shape of a banana peel, the result will be a fabric with the shape of a bowl or a boat. Sew several 'boats' together and you end up with a basketball. In other words, if you sew several pieces of rounded fabric together, the fabric will automatically billow. The billowing part of the fabric is called the camber. Clothes, for example, contain numerous cambers.

There are many ways to produce a camber in a sail. An obvious way is to add seams to the middle of the wings, having them run parallel to the spine of the kite. We have tried this but the final result was not very neat - ugly creases everywhere.

We then tried placing camber seams perpendicular to the wing spars. This was an improvement, but we still could not get rid of all the creases. Finally, we tried a radial camber - a pattern of seams resembling spokes of a wheel starting from the nose and fanning out to the trailing edge of the kite.

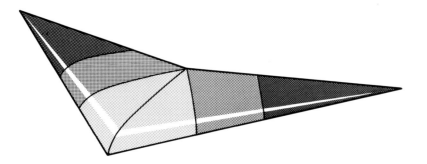

2 *...and perpendicular to the leading edges.*

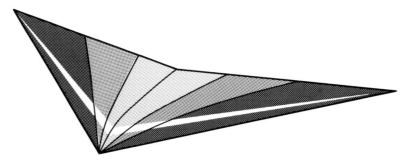

3 *The radial camber.*

This turned out to be the most satisfactory way to sew a camber in a kite sail. The most attractive aspect about this construction on a Speedwing was that no part of the camber had to be sewn onto the wing spars, this being the exact spot where creases would appear.

There are two ways to create a billow in the sail: by joining a straight piece of fabric to a round one, or by joining two rounded pieces of fabric together. The former is called an 'asymmetrical camber', the latter a 'symmetrical camber'. As the symmetrical camber is much easier to make and more accurate, this is the one we shall continue to describe.

CONSTRUCTION OF THE CAMBER

If you want your kite to have a camber, you first need to ask yourself a few questions. Where do you want the camber seams, how many will there be, how deep will they be, which direction will they face, will they be symmetrical or asymmetrical, etc. You can experiment for years to come in this still largely unexplored field!

Using the construction plan below, we will explain how we designed the camber when building one of the Speedwing Super prototypes. The construction plan serves no practical purpose for the making of the kite itself. However, it may come in handy one day when you want to design and build a different model of a cambered kite.

One of the Super prototypes we made consisted of two triangles measuring 68 x 106 x 132 cm each. We arbitrarily made camber seams in the sail:

two on the left, one in the centre seam and two on the right. On a cardboard template draw three lines, dividing the wing into three parts. At this point we wondered how deep the billowing should be and where it should be: right behind the front, halfway down the sail or close to the trailing edge?

We tried a camber of 1.5 cm per piece of fabric, i.e. 1.5 x 5 x 2 = 15 cm. This kite is as round as a tomato!

We estimated the deepest point of the curvature to be about one fourth of the nose, or 17 cm.

Draw a line from this point (D) to the wing tips, point C. This line will determine where the deepest billowing should come on the length of the template from where the camber lines and the deepest billow-lines cross. Draw a straight 15 mm line to point E.

Then comes the difficult bit: making a smooth camber line. With a thin fibreglass rod connect the two points in an offhand, curved line. With a Stanley knife cut out the camber along this line. Using a file, even out the rough edges to give it a smooth curve. If the camber is not deep (e.g. 5 mm on a 1 m long seam), do not bother to use a fibre glass rod for the curved line. Simply draw a straight line and cut out the camber along it. A kink will appear at point E but this will disappear once the kite is finished.

There is still one more problem to solve: a *concave* seam naturally remains in the cardboard next to where the *convex* seam was cut out. Here too we require a convex camber by lightly marking the corner points of the

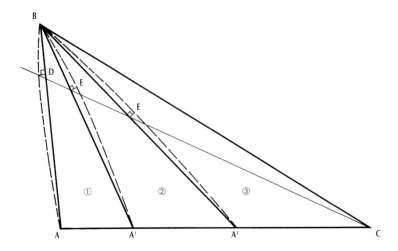

4 *Camber-seams in the Speedwing Super prototype.*

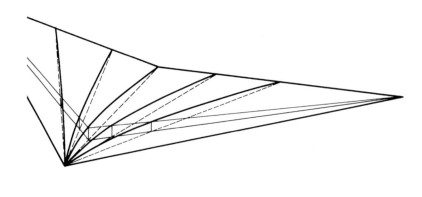

5 *Three-dimensional projection of a Speedwing camber.*

concave-seam template onto the spinnaker. Remove this template and lay the corresponding template (with the convex seam) upside down on the fabric. By definition this template should fit exactly onto the corner marks. Simply follow the edges of the template with a pencil. Add 6 mm to all camber seams (slide the template 6 mm further down the fabric) and cut them out. Because the fabric tends to billow here, a flat stitched seam is the obvious stitching method to use. A double flat stitched seam is better, but more difficult. Because the camber seam is symmetrical, you can easily place both sail panels on top of each other and glue them together. Use rubber-cement (double-sided tape is fine too). Sewing without gluing does not work very well - the end of the seam may end up uneven. Always sew the camber seams onto each other first (including flat stitching) and then the trailing edge seam so that this is kept free from obstructions in order for a piece of cord to be later threaded through.

If you are planning to make several kites of similar dimensions, it is worthwhile to add the camber-seams to all the templates. You can even consider including the hems in the templates as well. All you then have to do is lay the template onto the fabric, cut it out and start sewing. This is how professional kite workshops produce their kites.

A camber not only enhances the performance of Speedwings - Gizmos, Dykehoppers and Zipps all benefit from adding one. In fact, the performance of almost any kite improves considerably with a billowing sail.

SILENCING
A camber reduces the noise of a kite such as the Speedwing. We are not sure why this is, but we think it has to do with the increase in tension on the trailing edge of the kite. Another possibility is that the sail flaps less because of less turbulence in the airflow.

Tensioning the trailing edge of a kite makes the kite completely silent. You can do this by sewing some spinnaker hemming-band onto the trailing edge very tightly. Wrinkles will appear on the trailing edge because while you are sewing, you keep the hem tensioned as the machine transports the fabric. Commercial Speedwings are produced in this manner. But there is an easier way to tension the trailing edge: thread a cord through its hem. Tension lines like these can be found in the foresails of sailing boats as well as in windsurfing sails. Opinion differs as to the usefulness of this line, but in the case of kites they are indispensable.

The tension line is added as follows: first finish the kite but do not put the

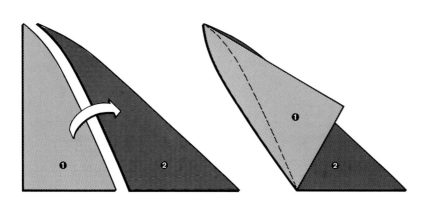

6 *Transfering camber onto next template.*

frame in yet. With a darning needle thread a piece of line of 20 kg breaking strength through the hem. Start anywhere between two stitches and work your way towards one of the wing spars. Upon reaching the wing pocket, push the needle right through the Dacron or Kevlar. Take the line out of the needle's eye and make a knot. Do the same at the other end then slightly tension the line and spread out the wrinkles along the trailing edge. Go fly the kite and listen carefully: if you still hear a flapping noise, tension the line a little more. Be careful not to exert too much pull on the line as this may prevent the kite from flying at all. This works perfectly, even with Speedwings without cambers (such as the one in our first book).

Finally some notes about the relation between bridle-adjustment and noise. A kite bridled too *high* will be noisy (it either flaps, makes a humming noise or sounds like a chain saw) even if it has a camber in its nose and a line in its trailing edge. So always adjust the bridle properly before adjusting the tension line on the trailing edge. As you lower the bridle clips, the pitch as well as the volume of the noise should decrease. Upon reaching the ideal bridle position, the kite should pull at its strongest and the trailing edge become quiet.

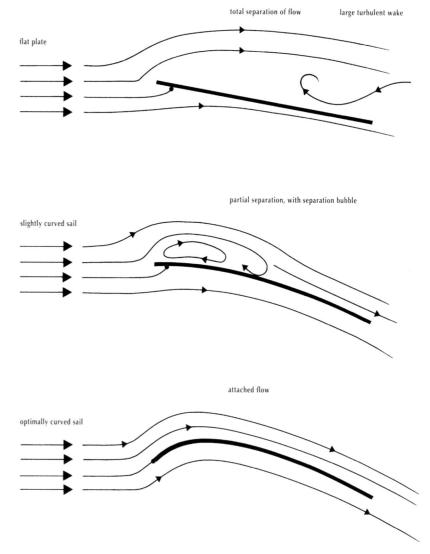

7 *Airflow patterns around various sail-profiles.*

6 THE BRIDLE

The correct setting of the bridle is what differentiates a good kite from a bad one, an experienced pilot from a beginner. It has taken us fifteen years to understand how this works - it will take you less than fifteen minutes.

Bridling a kite is a difficult skill to learn, but once you understand how it works, it is actually dead easy. Just to be perfectly clear, let us begin with the fundamental question: What is a bridle?

The bridle connects the kite to the control lines. It is a collection of lines with attachment points - usually clips - for the control lines. Every stunt kite has at least two control lines, so a bridle also consists of two parts: one for the left and one for the right side of the kite.

The bridle also distributes the pull of a kite over a number of points so that the pressure on the frame of the kite is evenly distributed. Generally speaking, the weaker the frame of the kite, the more bridle attachment points it will have. This is why, for example, the Sputnik 4 - a completely sparless kite - needs no less than 52 attachment points to distribute traction forces. The bridle also determines the position of the kite in relation to the air stream. By adjusting the clips on a bridle, the angle of attack of the wind on the sail changes. An exception to this rule is the Flexifoil and its cousins, where the wing profile determines the correct position of the kite when airborne. Thus there is no bridle whatsoever. Finally, the bridle makes it possible to control a kite, but more about that later.

We have distinguished between Speedwing-like kites (spineless kites) with a three-point bridle, regular 'swept-wing' delta kites with a four- or five-point bridle and kites without any frame. In the past few years, a clever system has been developed enabling flyers to make better turns with their kites no matter what sort of bridle the kite may have. We shall first explain this clever invention before discussing the three respective bridle categories in turn.

BETTER TIGHT-TURNING CHARACTERISTICS

Experience has taught us that the lower the bridle setting, the better the stunt kite turns. By 'better' we mean smaller, quicker turns without losing pressure or flapping sails.

We have also learned that you cannot continue adjusting the bridle lower and lower: the kite will eventually experience no lift at all or it will

1 A Speedwing flying straight up. The distance between the bridle-clip and the nose is 70 cm.

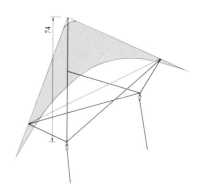

2 A sharp turn to the left. Now the distance between the bridle-clip and the nose is 74 cm. The angle of attack becomes steeper and the air-pressure on the sail is maintained.

just keep spinning, refusing to fly straight.

What we are looking for is a bridle which is automatically adjusting itself: a low setting during turns and a more moderate setting for straight line flying. Fortunately such a bridle does exist.

THREE-POINT BRIDLE

The bridle of a Speedwing is constructed differently from that of a 'normal' kite such as the Spin-off. Actually it does not have a spine to attach the bridle to. The Germans (Eric Heid, Thomas Erfurth and Harald Schlitzer) who invented the Speedwing came up with a three-point bridle: two attachment points at the spreader connectors and one attachment point at the nose. The trick of this bridle lies in the ring located halfway between the nose and the clips.

Due to this ring the top part of the bridle does not run in a straight line from the bridle clip to the nose. If a flyer manoeuvres the kite to the left, something interesting happens: the pull on the right bridle clip decreases, the dent in the uppermost part of the left bridle disappears and the connection between the nose and the left clip becomes a straight line. Hold the kite in front of you and try it - you will see it happen before your eyes.

3 Two ways to bridle a
kite. Left: the standard
bridle; right: the 'turbo'
bridle.

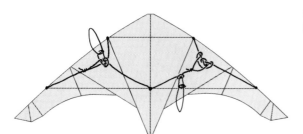

4 Connecting cord
in the top half of the
bridle.

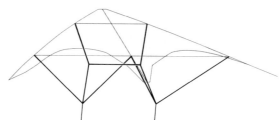

The disappearing of the dent causes this leg of the bridle to become longer. With a small Speedwing the difference is 4 cm: when the kite flies straight, the distance between the clips and nose is about 70 cm, when it turns, 74 cm. Since the lower part of the bridle remains the same during these turns the kite's bridle setting is 'automatically' adjusted lower during turns than when flying straight. This is the reason why a Speedwing can make such tight turns without losing pressure or dropping out of the sky.

By adjusting the ring on the bridle, it is possible to change the effectiveness of this automatism. If the kite pulls adequately when it flies straight but slackens during turns, the central ring has to be shifted lower, away from the nose. If the kite turns well but is hard to pull out of tight loops and back into straight line flying, the ring has to be shifted higher, towards the nose. After making adjustments to the central ring, the setting of the bridle clips needs to be optimized again.

WITH A SPINE

The bridle of a regular stunt delta with a spine usually consists of two three-leg bridles on each wing-half. On each half, one line is attached to the central cross-joint, one to the upper spreader connector and one to the bottom spreader connector. Altogether - since the central point is joint - it is a five-point bridle.

We chose to use one continuous line from the top spreader to the cross-joint and a short fixed line (the 'outhaul') from bottom spreader to bridle clip. In this way, the angle of attack is easily regulated by shifting the clip along the continuing line. But the opposite is also possible: a long line from top spreader via the bridle clip to the lower spreader. The short line then runs from the cross-joint to the clip.

In theory, it is better to make the bridle lines as long as possible. The pressure is then perpendicular to the surface of the kite causing less stress on the kite-frame. In particular the bottom spreaders run the risk of breaking when a short bridle is used.

In practice bridles are not made too long either, because not only do they tend to get caught on the wing tips of the kite, but they are usually made from heavy line. Longer lines, therefore, mean additional weight as well as drag at an unfavourable place - i.e. directly on the kite.

During our experiments, we came up with a bridle where the long, continuous line is approximately as long as the leading edge spars. The short bridle line is approximately 60 per cent of this length.

If the outhaul is lengthened, the clips will come closer together. Generally speaking, it is difficult to make quick manoeuvres when kites are bridled this way. This is only logical, when you come to think of it, because the pull is concentrated on the middle of the kite. When the kite is being steered it cannot lean enough into the wind, yet this is exactly what you would want a kite to do to make turns.

If the outhaul is shortened, the attachment points of the control lines will be too far apart and the kite will react as quick as lightning - often too quick. Moreover this way of bridling does not support the centre of the kite and puts a lot more stress on the bottom spreader.

Try our experiment bridle. The short bridle line is made 10 cm shorter and a cord with five knots at 5 cm intervals is attached to the attachment points on the leading edge. The length of the bridle can be adjusted by making a lark's

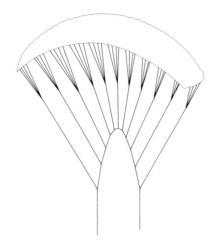

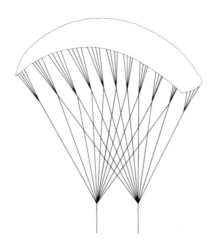

5 The arch bridle: for kites such as the Krypton-S and Sputnik.

6 The cross bridle. The kite is supported (almost) entirely by lines from each bridle point.

7 The conventional bridle causes an ugly kink to appear in the middle of the kite when it turns. We use it only on the Piraña.

head behind one of the five knots. Do not forget to adjust the clip on the main line whenever you shift the short bridle line. Indeed, this sort of experimenting works best with two people. Use sign language with your partner so that you do not have to run back and forth. A more professional method is to use two-way radios.

Now for the connecting cord. If you tie a cord between the left and right bridles halfway up the bridle line between the upper spreader and the clip, a dent will appear similar to the one on a Speedwing. This connecting cord functions exactly like the magical ring on a Speedwing bridle: it increases the angle of attack of the wind on the surface of the kite as it turns. Again, this makes the kite go faster as it turns while still maintaining a strong pull. By varying the length of the cord, the kite is affected in various ways. The shorter the cord, the more violent the reaction of the kite. Obviously the cord cannot be made too short; the right half of the bridle must be able to slacken when you pull on the left side.

Another variation is a shifting bridle. The bridle is not fixed at the top spreader, but runs through ringlets. When you pull right the bridle will shift a few centimetres to the right. This sets the right bridle lower and creates

tighter right turns. Pull left and the bridle will shift back.

A final alternative is the 'turbo bridle' we discovered on the *Big and Easy* Stunt Kite from the US. The bridle consists of four lines of equal length. Each line is 0.8 times the length of the leading edge spar. These separate 10 cm loops are used for connecting the bridle to the kite (Cf. Figure 3 on page 23 and El Macho construction plans). With the turbo-bridle this type of kite reacts even more efficiently than with any other available kind.

SPARLESS KITES

The bridle of sparless kites serves two functions: to establish the angle of flight and to maintain the kite's shape. The 'primary' and 'secondary' bridles perform these functions respectively.

The **primary bridle** consists of two, three or four short lines per profile (lines three and four are absent on some S-profiles). In order to fine-tune the sparless kite, all these lines have to be adjusted, which means quite a lot of work. Fortunately one only has to vary the length of the first line (at the opening where the air enters). See details of the construction plans for the Sputnik: other sparless kites are adjusted in the same way.

8 *A loop instead of a clip attached to the bridle prevents wear and tear.*

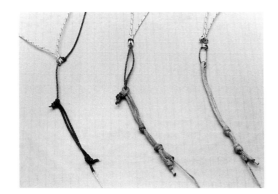

9 *The 'experiment' bridle.*

The **secondary bridle** transfers the power of the kite to the two control lines. It has to maintain the arch-like shape of the sparless kite during straight-line flight and tight turns. In recent years, three methods of tying secondary bridle lines have appeared:

- The conventional bridle, such as the one on the Piraña. The shape of the left and right parts of this kite are maintained by a separate bundle of bridle lines. Since there is no transition between the left and right half of the bridle an ugly dent appears in the middle of the wing when the kite turns.

- The arch bridle, such as the one on a Sputnik 4. Here the secondary bridle lines hang on a parabola-shaped arch. The bridle resembles an upside down suspension bridge . By varying the length of the secondary bridle lines and their spacing on the arch, the shape of the kite can be altered. Few distortions will appear even in tight turns, and very little line is necessary, thus reducing parasitic drag. With this type of bridle there is no built-in limit to the amount of control-input. The flyer could over-steer and thereby collapse the kite.

- The cross bridle, invented by Peter Lynn for his Peel kite. The main feature of this bridle is that the kite consists of two complete sets of bridles: one for optimum turning to the left and one for optimum turning to the right. The kite does not even collapse when flown with one line. The kite maintains its perfect shape during both wide circles and tight turns. The disadvantage of this bridle, however, is that it possesses too many lines, creating considerable drag.

TIPS

Safety line: Tie a tight, thin line from one wing tip - via the bottom of the spine - to the other wing tip. This simple trick prevents the bridle lines from getting caught on the wing tips or on the whiskers. This is especially important during 'ground work' and some of the advanced kite manoeuvres such as the *Turtle*.

Wax: Some bridle lines slide away from where they have been set, while others become so tight that adjusting the lines means having to fiddle around with the bridle in the cold for half an hour. Dip a 15 cm section of the bridle line where the knot is to come into melted beeswax to give the line the stiffness it needs.

Support: If the leading edge spars of a large kite bend too much, add an extra bridle line from the clip to the leading edge spar, right between the upper and lower spreaders. Make the line quite long so that it hangs slacker than the other bridle lines. This does not affect the kite's manoeuvrability.

Line instead of clip: Usually a clip is used for the bridle point, but bridle lines can also be attached directly to the control lines. Swivels are not necessary since modern kite lines do not twist. If you still have kites with aluminium rings as bridle points, we recommend you replace them. The pull of large, strong-pulling kites (e.g. El Macho and Sputnik), or stacks of kites, is far too strong for clips. Make a 10 cm long loop out of strong bridle-line and attach this with a lark's head to the bridle point instead of a clip. The control line is attached to this loop with a lark's head.

7 DESIGNING KITES YOURSELF

Kites are not designed by computers, they are rarely, if ever, tested in wind tunnels and they are certainly not 'developed' by thoughtful engineers. Kites are created by endlessly experimenting. Good kites are often the result of a stroke of luck, born in an instant as the builder absent-mindedly adjusts an old model.

It therefore comes as a surprise to us to see so many kite flyers actually standing in awe at kites designed by others. To them the 'Other Design' is something sanctifying, a kite they must copy without deviating a single millimetre from the original design.

The object of this book is, in fact, to render itself superfluous. We want you to become so enthusiastic and knowledgeable that in the near future you will not need any more advice from us. We want you to design kites yourself, make them yourself and fly them yourself, leaving this book to lead a solitary existence, collecting dust on a forlorn bookshelf.

But before you attain this independence, a few words of advice as to designing a kite yourself - in our opinion the most gratifying aspect of stunt kite flying.

The following advice is very general and does not apply to all situations and certainly not to all kite models. For designing and constructing sparless kites, see Chapter 9.

Advice No.1: Try to remain independent, no matter what other designs kite builders come up with. The builder of that fast kite you saw the other day? He was not a better flyer than you are - there was no specific reason why he used a 73.8 cm cross spar, he just happened to find one in his drawer. The concave shape of the trailing edge? He probably drew a line at random or made use of a soup bowl lying on the kitchen table. The length of the bridle lines? He probably made a wild guess and just used up some leftover line from an old spool. In all likelihood, there was simply no special reason for designing it the way he did, nor was there any use for a computer or calculator .

Advice No.2: Use a standard frame. Modern kite frames consist of carbon fibre rods. Carbon fibre is expensive, quite fragile and cannot be recycled: you will not want to waste it.

In Europe you will find a marvellous array of carbon fibre rods that come in metric sizes - you can save yourself a lot of money and frustration by using these rods as a starting-point for designing your kite.

Let us take the example of an enlarged Spin-off from our first book. The leading edges of the original Spin-off have an unfavourable length of 132 cm. The nearest standard rod size is 150 cm, so 18 cm is wasted. By increasing the size of the kite by 150/132 (with a calculator) you will have a kite with a standard 1.50 m rod fitting into the leading edge. Use 1.50 m rods for the lower spreader as well. Saw the rod into two 75 cm lengths. The spine, some 75 cm long, comes from a 1.25 rod, which leaves 50 cm for the upper spreader - a perfect size. It does not really matter if the spine turns out to be slightly longer, or the spreader slightly shorter, or the other way round.

But remember, if you make a kite bigger or smaller, the relative weight of the kite and its rigidity will change; thus it will have to sustain - or need - more wind or less wind.

Advice No.3: Manipulate the shape of the nose. Sometimes you may find rods falling short of the desired length. No problem, simply cut off a piece of material from the nose and sew onto a new piece of webbing. As a result the pockets of the spine and leading edges will become much shorter and the rods will suddenly fit in. This nose trick works only with kites that have upper and lower spreaders. The upper spreader keeps the nose extended. A kite such as the Zipp, which does not have an upper spreader, is more critical as far as this is concerned. A wide nose will make the upper half of a Zipp slacken, thereby destabilising it somewhat in tight turns.

Advice No.4: Small modifications can sometimes lead to considerable changes. A few practical examples: without a tension cord to its trailing edge, the Speedwing Super prototype was no better than the original Speedwing. With a tension cord, however, the Super gained at least 30 per cent more power.

At first, La Hembra's test model had 2 cm more billowing on its leading edges. This turned out to be slightly too much; a small 'dent' appeared in the sail and it would not fly.

Advice No.5: Do not make your prototype kites too small. Small kites are more sensitive to design flaws and, in general, need more wind than larger kites. Moreover, small kites react more extremely to modifications - so extreme in fact that you may just miss the correct adjustment point.

What is small? A kite such as the Spin-off is considered small when its leading edge rods are 1.25 m, medium when these are 1.50 m and large when 2 m long.

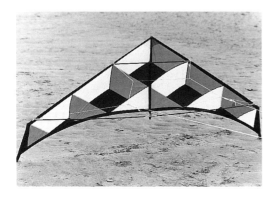

1 A high Aspect Ratio: The Dykehopper.

2 Hawaiians *have a low Aspect Ratio.*

3 A failed experiment: the Pyramid *looks great but flies terribly.*

A kite without a spine, such as the Speedwing, is considered small when its leading edge rods are 82.5 cm, medium when these are 1 m and large when 1.25 m long.

Advice No.6: Increase the size of a kite gradually - do not start with a kite with a 4 m wing span, for example. First get to know the forces a kite can be exposed to. Generally, it is easier to increase power by stacking kites rather than making a kite twice as large. See Appendix VI, *'Stacking Kites'*.

Advice No.7: Do not design a kite from scratch. Let us assume there is a kite you are almost satisfied with, only you would like it to become more man-oeuvrable (give the sail more tension), launch more easily (add a camber in the sail), fly better in turbulent winds (add gauze to the sail), etc. Through subtle alterations in design an aerobatic kite can become specialised in carrying out extraordinary manoeuvres. Here are some details:

Tensioning the sail
Kites with highly tensioned sails fly faster and pull harder than those with billowing sails. You can, therefore, increase the performance of an existing kite by lengthening the cross spars with the help of short carbon fibre ex-tenders. The kite will become flatter and more difficult to launch. The *Wolken-stürmer 101* is a good example here. These kites are sensitive on making turns; a sudden manoeuvre can cause them to stall and drop uncontrollably to the ground.

Top angle
Kites with a large top angle, kites with a wide wingspan and a high Aspect Ratio (see chapter on 'Sparless Kites') fly faster than more quadrangular, squat kites with pointed noses.

Kites with wide wingspans often have over-steering problems. Because the mass is distributed over a large area, once a turn has started the kite cannot abruptly stop. Such large kites are not really suitable for precision flying and are often too fragile for power-kiting.

Spine length
Kites with a lengthened spine are stable and extremely reliable. They can be launched easily, fly slower and track better than kites with trailing edges that more or less extend from one wing tip to another in a single, curved line.

Sail shapes
- The traditional Hawaiian kite is hardly flown anymore. The large surface area in the sail at the wing tips is difficult to tension. This slows down the kite and causes it to lose pressure when making turns.
- Sail-battens extending beyond the trailing edge keep the sail tensioned; ne-

4 *The* Magnum Opus *is a good example of a modern stunt kite: high Aspect Ratio, light frame and no less than ten sail-battens and whiskers.*

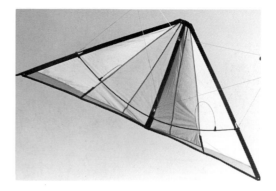

5 *Gauze has been sewn on to the trailing edge of this model for noise-reduction.*

6 *The circles indicate vulnerable points on kites.*

cessary in the case of slim, high Aspect Ratio kites.

- Kites with a convex trailing edge produce less noise than those with a straight one.
- Furling some sail at the tip of the kites will pre-load the tips of the leading edge rods, thereby tensioning the trailing edge of the kite. This prevents the sail from flapping.
- Kites with cambers in their sails are easier to launch, they pull harder and make less noise than flat kites.
- The camber in a sail ensures that the billowing of the sail takes on the shape of an airfoil.
- Adding gauze to the kite's sail reduces power considerably without altering its flight performance.
- Gauze panels in the wing tips - such as in La Hembra - stabilize kites when stalling.

Frame
- Kites with a rigid frame retain their shape better in strong winds, they fly faster and are quieter than similar kites with weaker frames, though they tend to be heavier and thus need more wind than lighter designs.
- Bear in mind that when enlarging a kite its frame becomes relatively more flexible.

Sail-battens
- Sail-battens, stand-offs or whiskers (several of which are sometimes used on each wing-half), are indispensable for reliable flight-performance. Without stand-offs, the same kite could easily lose its balance in tight turns - especially at the edges of the wind window, causing the kite to flutter to the ground.
- Do not allow the stand-offs to tension the fabric so much that wrinkles appear. If

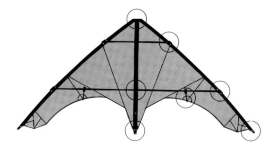

7 The batten between the upper spreader and whisker prevents the whisker from creating ugly creases in the sail. Here a Powerhouse Team.

8 This whisker functions as a camber inducer: the whisker pushes the sail-batten to the rear so that the sail billows.

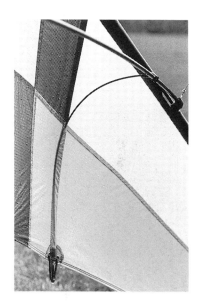

there is a deep indentation in the trailing edge of the kite, stand-offs will face the nose and cause unattractive wrinkles to appear. If that happens you can add extra battens between the upper spreader and stand-offs.
- Make sure the stand-offs' ends protrude as little as possible - control lines can easily get caught on protruding ends.

PRACTICAL TIPS

1 Take your time. A complicated design can take years to perfect. Do not make more than one change to your kite at a time. If you make several changes on a prototype in a single session, you can never be sure which alteration affected the design.

2 Do not work too accurately. Yes, you read this correctly! Especially when building a large kite, there is no need to work accurately to the last millimetre. Rounding off half a centimetre will not make any difference. In fact you save time by not working accurately - leaving you time to make a second prototype in the same weekend. In this way you can conduct experiments much faster. One problem with this advice, however, is that you must know where accuracy does count and where it does not.

3 Think beforehand where the kite is likely to suffer damage. Usually it will be at the nose, the wing tips, the lower end of the spine, the sleeve of the spine near the cross-joint and at the bridle-attachment point. Reinforce these problem spots with Kevlar and/or Dacron.

4 Record in detail the results of your experiments. Keep a small notebook at hand in which you can jot down information on the circumstances under which you are experimenting (wind speeds, wind direction, location, temperature, precipitation etc.), the changes you have made in a design and how the kite 'reacted' to these alterations. As you scribble your notes you may not see the usefulness of this, but weeks later as you thumb through your notebook like golfers do, you will often come across the clear coherence of your experiments. This sometimes leads to a classic 'Eureka'!

When you have finally designed a fantastic new kite, it is time to ponder the following. Do I keep the design to myself? Sell it to a shop? Start manufacturing it? Publish an article about it in a kite magazine? Get a patent?

Publishing an article is probably the best thing you can do. Everyone will acknowledge the designer and many can benefit from it. A patent is only feasible for companies with huge financial reserves. So far only the Flexifoil company has managed to protect its design effectively through a patent. Kites invented by smaller, sometimes brilliant kite-designers are being indiscriminately copied all the time, rarely with any legal consequences.

8 AEROBATICS

There are windshield wipers and aerobatic kite flyers. The first group consists of those who fly their kites left and right in endless monotony. We will not deal with them here. The second group consists of pilots who have the ability to caper their kites around the sky in a most astounding manner.

The US is the cradle of 'complex' stunt kite flying. Many of the tricks we shall be discussing would never have been invented had there been no stunt kite competitions in the US. A healthy dosage of rivalry seems almost a prerequisite for extracting the ultimate creativeness from stunt kite flyers. You will find detailed information regarding competition flying in Appendix VIII (page 109) under the heading 'S.T.A.C.K.'.

There are literally hundreds of figures and they are hard to keep track of. But fortunately, S.T.A.C.K. publishes an annual list of the ever-increasing new figures in which each figure is given a name and number. Compulsory figures for competitions are selected from this list. The *KiteFlight* computer programme keeps track of as many figures as possible; the figures appear on the screen and are analysed. The level of difficulty of these figures is not high; with the basic flying techniques described in *Stunt Kites - To Make and Fly*

you can go a long way and we will teach you how to score higher with your compulsory figures. This is followed by an introduction to some tricks that can turn any kite demonstration into a spectacular show.

To make the manoeuvres more comprehensible, we provide pictograms along with the descriptions. These explain how to use your hands for the desired effect. But remember, you cannot learn how to perform the tricks merely by reading and analysing the figures - you have to go out to the flying site and sweat it out for hours on end like everyone else.

Not all kites are appropriate for aerobatic flying. The Flexifoil and Sputnik do not have the qualities to perform all manoeuvres, though they are capable of functioning in other ways (see page 37). Traditional diamond-shaped kites such as the Peter Powell and Ace are virtually useless, and stunt kites such as the Zipp and Speedwing have only limited possibilities. What you need is a top-model such as a Little Sister, Phantom, Powerhouse Team, Trickster or Tracker. These and a dozen other kites with a price tag of US $200 and above have proven to be excellent kites for the purpose. We prefer our own creation, La Hembra. She is easy to launch from any position, can float on her back with stability and perform a snappy turtle with predictability. Aerobatic flying works best in light winds when you can walk forward and backwards at ease. In 4 Beaufort winds you have to run like mad towards the kite to land. For performing aerobatic manoeuvres, it is advisable to fly with short (25 - 30 metres), thin (50 - 75 kg breaking strength) lines.

And now, with special thanks to the dual-line artist and uncrowned Scheveningen champion, Richard Zandberg, here is the promised enumeration:

Speed control

In figures such as the 'steps down' the kite tends to go too fast to round all corners properly before hitting the ground, especially when short lines are used. Slow down the kite by taking a few steps forward - the corners become smoother and suddenly you will find ample time to complete the manoeuvre. Speed control is also important when performing other figures. To perform the circle in the 'circle in a square' manoeuvre nice and round, you should take a few gradual steps towards the kite as it is flying down, then take a few steps back as it is flying the upwards part of the circle. The entire figure looks at its best when the kite flies at constant speeds throughout the manoeuvre. More control is necessary when performing the 'team rainbow'. All four kites remain

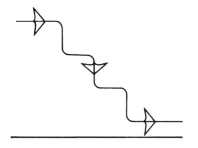

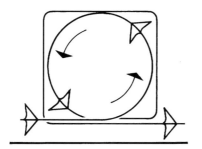

1 *Practicing speed control: the 'steps down' manoeuvre.*

2 *Circle in a square.*

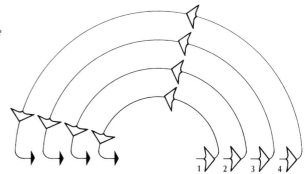

3 *'Team-rainbow': half of the team walks forward, the other half backwards.*

next to each other when flying an arch. This can only be done if Pilot 1 takes quick steps forward, Pilot 2 takes slow steps forward while Pilots 3 and 4 respectively take slow and quick steps backwards.

Sharp corners and Snap-turns

Short, tight corners are made by jerking the arms aggressively as the kite is steered. Several variations are possible. In the diagrams the figures are shown together with the appropriate movements of the upper and lower arms. The kite is not flown with outstretched arms, but with the elbow bent at an angle of approximately 90°.

1 **Pull-push-turn:** This is how the kite is instinctively controlled even if the flyer has not done any homework on stunt kite flying. A strong pull on one line makes the kite turn in the desired direction. The strength of the pull and its length determine the angle of the turn. Intuition will help you find the precise 90° angle for a square. The properties of a pull-push-turn are: a good recognisable initialisation of the turn, followed by a weak return to a straight line. Some kites will remain turning (over-steering) slightly longer.

2 **Push-pull-turn** works the other way around. Begin with a strong forward motion - like a boxing punch. This starts the kite rotating. Then pull the line with a jerk straight into the desired direction. This technique is difficult, but is useful for complex figures such as the 'octagon' with 45° turns. The push-pull technique accentuates the end of a turn, reducing the risk of over-steering because the kite is immediately pulled back into the correct direction.

3 The **push-push-turn** is mainly used in strong winds and for team flying because of its delaying effect. This smooth turn can be somewhat pepped

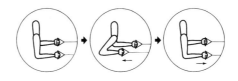

4 *Pull-push-turn: the standard kite control movement.*

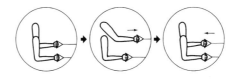

5 *Push-pull-turn: like a boxing punch.*

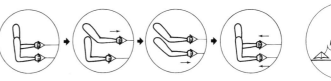

6 *Push-push-turn: reduces speed.*

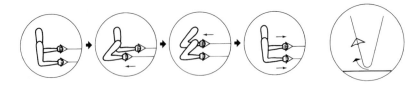

7 Pull-pull-turn: the agressive kite control movement.

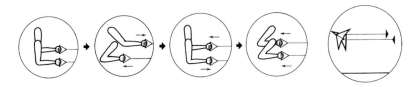

8 Snap-turn: for special tricks.

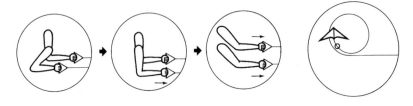

9 In a stall, the air current stops following the contour of the sail and the kite comes to a standstill.

up by simultaneously jerking both arms after the turn. By making a push-push turn of 90° upwards at the end of a groundsweep, followed by a few steps in the direction of the kite, it is easy to land the kite. Even a Speedwing Super can land on its wing tips with this technique.

4 The ***pull-pull-turn*** creates such radical turns that it may affect your precision performance. In light winds the pull-pull-turn technique is combined with walking backwards because after the turn you need to stretch out your arms again without reducing the kite's speed. This technique is also used to perform aggressive power dives as shown in the Figure.

5 The ***combination*** or ***snap-turn*** is the most subtle and frequently used technique in advanced aerobatics. In this manoeuvre, the kite actually stops flying. This is done by giving a strong pull with one hand while pushing with the other, immediately followed by bringing both hands together again. What is important is not how far you move your arms but the speed of the movement; the movements of your wrists are sufficient. The kite stops in mid-flight because the air current around its wings is totally disrupted and it begins to revolve on its axis. When the nose of the kite points into the desired direction, both lines are given a tug. With this technique you can fly the tightest squares. A 'clicking' sound is heard after each turn the kite makes. With a snap-turn, you can fly the kite horizontally and, without changing altitude, turn it 180° around very quickly.

Stall

When a kite stalls, the air current stops following the sail of the kite and it hangs in a bell of turbulent air. In reality, the kite already stalls in a snap-turn except that it tends to continue spinning. To make the kite stall in a stable manner, first make a quick loop, immediately followed by a push-push motion. At the same moment, step forward. The reverse steering input stops the spinning action of the kite and drives the wind from the sail. By walking forward, the situation does not change. The trick is then to keep the kite motionless with its nose facing up: calmly walk forward (depending on the wind speeds) and make subtle steering movements. Much depends on the stability of the kite. Some models begin to spin out of control, others take off even if you run forward. As a rule, setting the bridle at a lower angle solves the problem. In an ideal situation, a stalled kite can be made to drift down backwards from a high altitude until it lands on its wing tips.

Snap-stall

If you want to give a good kite demonstration, you should be able to stall the kite completely, preferably with as little rotation of the kite as possible. In light winds this is an easy thing to do: by suddenly giving the lines the entire length of your arms, the kite comes to a complete standstill. Because the air current around the wings is not disrupted too much, the kite soon flies away again. But this motion is not snappy enough. A precise snap-stall is done by performing several snap-turns one after another with wrist (10 - 15 cm) moves, left-right and right-left. As a result of the contradictory com-

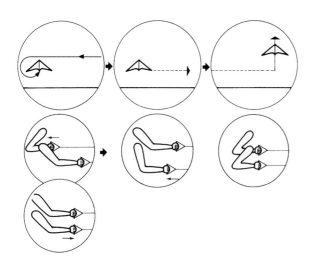

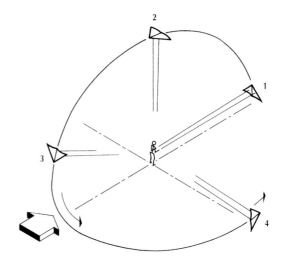

10 A slide *manoeuvre: the kite glides horizontally across the wind window.*

11 *The* 360° *manoeuvre: a nice manoeuvre to perform on windless days.*

12 *The* up & over *manoeuvre: the trick to perform if you want to show off.*

mands, the kite stops flying. If the kite keeps following a zig-zag course instead of stalling, your wrist movements are not snappy enough.

Slide

In a 'slide' the kite flies perpendicularly to the normal flight direction. The slide works as follows: the kite flies horizontally towards the edge of the wind window. With a downward push-push loop of 270° the kite stalls, but because of the loop's speed the kite immediately retrieves the desired sideways speed towards the centre of the wind window. The nose of the kite faces up but the kite glides (slides) sideways as a quad-line kite would. This is done by taking a few steps forward while tensioning the lines as little possible and by keeping the kite at an angle in the wind. The wing facing the gliding direction is a bit closer to the flyer than the other wing. By giving both lines a little tug, the kite flies forward normally again.

Three-sixty

The kite is flown low above the ground, 360° around the flyer. This manoeuvre is done for fun during a kite festival when the winds have died down. To make

the kite fly around yourself, 'wind' is created by walking. The technique of walking is important: look frequently over your shoulder and do not walk faster than necessary to keep the kite in the air. This means observing the kite's behaviour carefully; as soon as it starts to hang at a slight angle or moves sideways it stalls. Then it is time to increase speed. Keep walking perpendicularly away from the kite, which will make a large circle while you make a small one. If you want to perform this manoeuvre with wind, you must walk in a spiral pattern rather than a circular one (Cf. Figure 11).

The 360 degree flight can be performed in winds up to 8 km/h.

Up & over

The sequel to the 'three hundred sixty' works as follows. Bring the kite up above your head as high as possible as you walk backwards (In the Figure from 1 to 2). Make sure you stretch out your arms completely at the highest point. Get ready for the critical moment: pull the kite through the zenith and sprint forward. The objective of this manoeuvre is to maintain tension on the lines while the kite flies down against the (light) wind (in the Figure from 2 to 3). Keep flying until you reach the ground, from there finish the three-sixty (from 3 to 4). Try this in winds up to 5 km/h at the most.

Fly away

In light winds you have to constantly walk backwards in order to keep the kite airborne. At a certain moment, however, you cannot go any further because of obstacles such as a ditch, a wall, a fence, a nuclear plant etc. So how do you return to where you started without having to land the kite? Simply let the kite fly back to where it started from! From the highest point, do a power dive as you quickly walk down wind. The kite should not fly down vertically as in a normal power dive but should sail away from you in a horizontal downwind gliding-dive. Keep the lines tensioned as little as possible, just enough to control the kite's course. As a matter of principle, a kite glides faster in the 'correct' direction than the wind does. If you walk too fast, the kite may end up in an annoying reversed-turtle - a difficult position to retrieve the kite from. If you walk too slowly, however, the kite continues power-diving and crashes, but when done properly some 20 to 30 metres of ground can be gained with each gliding-dive. Often walking back a mere five metres is enough to fly the kite high again. The process is then repeated. Performing three-sixties is another excellent way to gain ground, especially if you are flying a kite not stable enough to do a gliding-dive.

Helicopter

The 'helicopter' is similar to the 'glider'. Once again, begin with the kite in the zenith, though this time a power dive is initiated with a snap-turn. After the snap do not bring your hands back together but immediately give a lot of line with some 30 cm or so difference in length. Next, walk downwind at the same speed as the wind. The kite - while circling - will glide down horizontally to the ground.

LANDING AND LAUNCHING

You have no doubt mastered the technique of landing and launching your kite by positioning it on its wing tips (*Stunt Kites - To Make and Fly*, page 26). Now you can learn some other ways so you need never walk back to the kite to set it upright again.

Leading edge landing

This is easy to do. Fly the kite low above the ground until you have passed the centre of the wind window; steer it at a 45° angle toward the ground and land

it. Use a push-turn and take some of the speed out of the kite to lessen the impact on the carbon fibre rods. To launch the kite from this position, slowly pull the control line on the wing facing up until the kite tilts towards you. Tilt it until it looks as if it will tip forward. Keeping your hands in the same position (approximately 50 cm difference in length) give both lines a tug. The wing tip will scrape the ground for a moment, then the kite will take off. The nearer the kite is to the centre of the wind, the harder it is to perform this trick.

This method does not work with all kite models; if it doesn't work for your kite, try the next method.

Flip-over

If a kite does not fly away from the leading edge position, you can park the kite on its wing tips by feeding some line to the uppermost wing so that the kite leans backwards. Then pull on the line of the lower wing: some kites need a strong tug. The kite will then stand upright on its wing tips which remain planted on the ground. From this position the kite can easily be re-launched. Take extra care when doing a flip-over because the rods can break easily.

Wing tip landing and Wing tip drag

Steer the kite diagonally down from the upper left corner to the ground. First practise this at the edge of the window. Later, move towards the centre of the wind window and try it there. To do this manoeuvre, fly the kite one metre above the ground and make a push-turn to the right followed by a snap-turn to the left. The kite will stall in a 45° position and descend, digging its right wing tip firmly into the ground. Allow the kite to lean backwards by slightly feeding the upper (left) line (if you do not do this the kite will take off again) and keep controlling the kite with the lower (right) line. By pulling this line, the kite will lean to the left. By feeding some line it returns to its original position - totally the opposite effect you would have expected. By pulling the upper line (left), the kite will take off. At the same time, you can feed the lower line quickly. In one movement, the kite will now switch from the right to the left wing tip. From this position you can launch the kite with a wing tip drag: the kite stands on its left wing tip at the right side of the window. Pull both lines and the kite will fly away horizontally. Make sure the kite does not gain altitude. Tension the upper line a bit more and let the kite drag its wing tip along the ground to the left. Upon reaching the opposite side of the window the entire manoeuvre can be repeated.

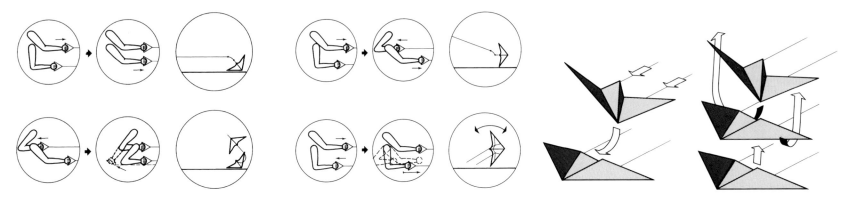

13 *A trick anyone can learn:* the leading-edge landing.

14 *The* wing tip landing *is a bit more difficult but easy to learn.*

15 Nose in, *just before the kite crashes into the ground it flips, landing on its belly.* Magic Carpet, *the kite floats horizontally away.*

Downward-loop landing

The kite flies parallel to the ground with a margin of roughly one wingspan. Make a downward-loop, wait until the nose of the kite faces upwards and make a short but strong snap-turn in the opposite direction. At that moment, take a few steps forward. The kite will land on both wing tips. If you start this manoeuvre too high (for fear of breaking the rods) the kite hangs far above the ground after the spin and forces you to dash forward to land it. If you spin the kite too low, however, it will crash.

The following tricks are more difficult to perform accurately; even experienced flyers risk failure when attempting these manoeuvres.

Nose in / Pancake

Fly the kite down vertically into the centre of the wind window. Depending on the wind's force you can walk forward to reduce speed. As you fly the kite, bring your arms to your sides. Just before the kite hits the ground, create a huge wave-like motion with both hands and arms, feed line simultaneously. At the same moment, take a few quick steps forward. Now the kite will not crash; instead to your surprise it turns its nose away and lands on its belly with its trailing edge facing the direction of the wind. If the 'belly-landing' does not work, the wind was probably too strong. This manoeuvre can be more snappy if you first give the kite a small tug just before feeding the line.

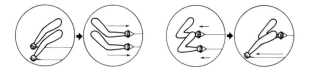

If the wind is too strong, the kite remains on its belly - the wind lifts it up and it ends up standing on one of its leading-edges instead.

Magic Carpet

A spectacular way to launch a kite in extremely light winds from the belly-landing is the so-called 'Magic Carpet'. Give both lines a short tug. The kite will then glide horizontally on its belly a couple of metres above the ground until the wind picks it up. In one single movement the kite returns to the correct position and flies away. Because the nose is pointing down there is the danger of the kite crashing immediately, the trick here is to keep a difference of 30 cm between your hands so that the kite has time to turn away. This manoeuvre, however, remains risky.

Turtle

Quickly steer the kite until it is right over your head; pump it to go further. Then, by throwing your hands up from your knees to above your head in one movement, feed the lines very quickly. The kite's nose will fling backwards

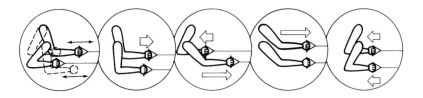

16 *Movements for the Axel.*

and the kite drift down on its reverse side with slack lines.

Let the kite drift down until it is a few metres above the ground. By feeding the kite more line, the nose leans back further. In one gradual motion, pull both hands towards your body and the kite will flip backwards.

Axel

This is a manoeuvre similar to the helicopter whereby the kite makes a horizontal loop parallel to the ground but right into the wind. The kite must stall, flip forward, turn 360° and flip backwards again. This is the most difficult manoeuvre in our bag of tricks:

1 Stall the kite positively with, for example, a snap-stall. The kite should remain hanging stably in the air, nose up.
2 Feed one of the lines (about 5 cm); the kite will remain stalled.
3 Give a short, snappy tug with the same hand you moved forward. At the same time feed plenty of line with the other hand.
4 Now feed the line you tugged first. The kite should now be doing the 'helicopter' manoeuvre with slack lines.
5 When you see the front of the kite appear, tension the lines. The wind will do the rest.

Tip: Except for feeding the lines, make all movements from the wrists only!

AEROBATICS IN TEAM FLYING

The KiteFlight programme includes, aside from S.T.A.C.K. figures for teams, several complete routines which have been flown during some of the World Cup competitions. High Performance, one of the top US teams, uses the above mentioned complex manoeuvres even in its routine.

Because some of these are three-dimensional, they do not show up on a flat computer screen. This is also true of some of the opening moves of the routines.

In team flying, you can make the kites stick to each other either by applying Velcro to the wing tips of the kites or by placing elastic bands on the wing tips

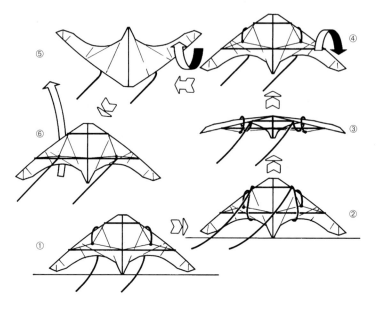

17 *The* broken yo-yo: *a spectacular way to launch a kite.*

into which the other kites can stick their wing tips. Attaching kites to each other works particularly well in the launching position. The Figure illustrates how team High Performance begins one of its ballet routines.

Team Shred, another team from the US, uses the following opening: Kite 1 stands with its nose stuck under the upper spreader of Kite 2. Like a quad-line kite, the two pilots fly their joint kites up, (with the kites in a vertical position). Sometime later Kite 3 appears and rams the two kites from below, separating them with full force.

Another strange phenomenon is the broken yo-yo launch. This manoeuvre needs a bit of preparatory work: place the grips on a ground stake and position the kite ready for launching. Now roll the kite forward with the nose between the two lines and keep turning it until the nose faces up again. You can now do two things: have someone support the kite in this position, or hook the lines onto the protruding upper cross-fittings at the leading edge. Return to the grips and launch the kite by pulling the lines carefully. The kite will drift up into the sky until the lines separate themselves from the cross-fittings. The kite will then flip over and make a 360° rotation until it returns to its normal position before flying away. The kite can also be 'wrapped' around its own

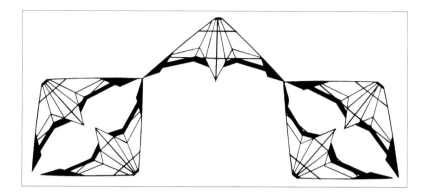

18 One of Team High Performance's launching positions.

19 Team Shred's method of launching joint kites.

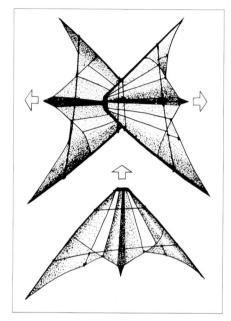

20 La Hembra performs all aerobatic tricks.

lines several times. Just make sure that the lines are wrapped around, away from the spine, somewhere between the connectors of the upper and lower spreaders.

MANOEUVRES WITH THE SPUTNIK AND THE FLEXIFOIL

Although it is difficult to make snappy turns with these two models, these kites were first used to perform the three-sixty and the up & over manoeuvres.

A well-adjusted Sputnik can perform excellent slides. In a stall the kite is easy to control and it can also land and take off again perfectly.

Balancing the kite on its wing tip is quite a spectacular sight - it collapses like an accordion but can also expand again and take off.

SKIPPING ROPE

It is easy to do a three-sixty using a large 10 ft Flexifoil with Ultra-light rods. By continuously flying the kite low anyone looking for a challenge can try skipping the rope by jumping between the lines!

9 SPARLESS KITES

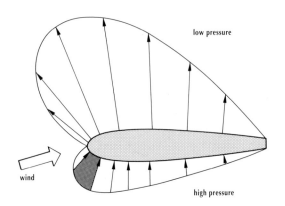

1 *The distribution of air-pressure on the wing profile. There is a strong low pressure area on the top of the kite and a high pressure area on the bottom of the kite. The indicated area shows where the high pressure is strongest: place the gauze opening here.*

2 *The banana-shape of a deformed sparless kite: too little volume and a too high Aspect Ratio.*

Sparless kites have a lot of advantages: they are seemingly unbreakable, lightweight, soundless, easy to enlarge or make smaller, less dangerous for bystanders and can be folded away into a small bag. But they also have disadvantages: they use a lot of fabric, they can take days to make, the bridles can get hopelessly tangled and if the kite crashes midwind, the inner seams can be torn open. Moreover, these kites are more sensitive to 'foul' winds than most stunt-delta kites are: in turbulent winds, for example, sparless kites can sometimes collapse unexpectedly.

Nevertheless, sparless kites - both the dual- and quad-line types - have become the workhorses for buggying; they are also popular as a power-source for kite-sailing. The greatest advantage of these kites on water is that they remain buoyant for a long time after crashing, whereas delta kites quickly get damaged in the surf.

Sputnik 4 is the best sparless kite in our collection. The construction of the kite is relatively simple, its wind range is surprisingly wide (up to 8 Beaufort winds) and it displays a stable (and rather frightening) pull. The first time you launch a Sputnik there will be only one thing you will want to do: get it down as fast as possible. What a brute force this kite has!

It was the challenge to equal the 'Peel' of Peter Lynn which caused us to develop Sputnik 4. In 1992 the 'Peel' became the sensation of the international flying scene and it is now considered by many to be the most appropriate kite for buggying and kite-sailing. But we will have to wait and see which kite emerges as the 'best' kite - the fact remains that the field of sparless kites is still in a development stage: many more variations, including quad-line kites are certain to appear at competitions in the coming years.

THE PROFILE

The Sputnik is sewn together with ribs of symmetrical profiles - the top and bottom curves being mirror images. We tried to select the lowest profile-drag possible to attain high speeds.

The 'thickness' of the profile is - after it has been stitched to the kite - about 15 per cent of the length of the profile. The thickness of the profile only partly determines the thickness of the kite in its totality. (See 'Number of Ribs', page 41).

The rear of the profile does not, as is customary in other sparless kites, taper off, but ends in a straight edge instead. The reasons for this are:
1 The shape of the trailing edges of well-known sparless kites such as the Flexifoil and Paraflex are very irregular. The fabric between the ribs has the tendency to billow out because of internal air pressure even when the profiles taper off towards the rear. The consequence: the trailing edge resembles a row of inflated plastic lunch bags.
2 Because the fabric on the trailing edge is 'rumpled' as opposed to the taut leading edge, the shape of the entire kite becomes distorted - the wing tips bend backwards and the kite ends up looking like a flying banana. When the tip-profile ends in a straight edge, however, the fabric at the back remains more taut and the banana-shape disappears.
3 The volume or the 'thickness' of the kite determines its sturdiness. The thicker the profiles of a kite, the more the kite retains its shape. For the sake of speed, we prefer profiles which are as thin as possible. By giving more 'body' to the rear half of the profile, the profile can, as a whole, become thinner without losing volume.

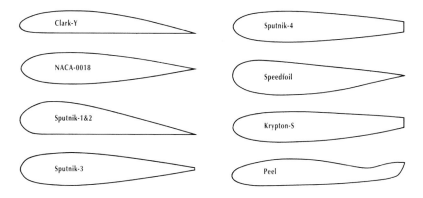

profiles																
base	Clark-Y		NACA-0018		Sputnik-1&2		Sputnik-3		Sputnik-4		Speedfoil		Krypton-S		Peel	
X %	Yb	Yo	Yb	Yo	Yb	Yo	Yb	Yo	Yb	Yo	Yb	Yo	Yb	Yo	Yb	Yo
0	3.5	3.5	0.0	0.0	8.8	6.1	0.0	0.0	0.0	0.0	0.0	0.0	0.0	0.0	0.0	0.0
2,5	6.5	1.6	3.9	3.9	11.7	2.4	3.7	3.7	3.4	3.4	4.2	6.2	2.5	3.5	4.5	2.2
5	7.9	0.9	5.3	5.3	13.6	0.6	5.3	5.3	4.9	4.9	6.2	7.6	5.0	5.0	5.6	2.9
10	9.6	0.4	7.0	7.0	16.0	0.0	7.0	7.0	6.5	6.5	8.0	9.3	6.6	6.6	6.7	3.9
20	11.4	0.0	8.6	8.6	17.4	0.0	8.3	8.3	8.0	8.0	8.9	11.1	8.2	8.2	9.0	4.3
30	11.7	0.0	9.0	9.0	16.6	0.0	8.3	8.3	8.5	8.5	7.8	11.5	8.6	8.6	10.1	4.2
40	11.4	0.0	8.7	8.7	14.9	0.0	8.0	8.0	8.4	8.4	6.7	11.3	8.6	8.6	9.9	4.0
60	9.2	0.0	6.8	6.8	10.4	0.0	6.5	6.5	7.5	7.5	4.4	9.1	8.1	7.2	7.8	3.2
80	5.2	0.0	3.9	3.9	5.0	0.0	3.8	3.8	5.5	5.5	2.2	4.4	7.3	4.0	5.1	1.5
100	0.0	0.0	0.0	0.0	0.0	0.0	0.7	0.7	3.0	3.0	0.0	0.0	6.0	0.0	8.8	-8.5

OTHER PROFILES

As far as we know, Sputniks 3 and 4 are the only sparless kites with a symmetrical profile. The most common Parafoil profiles are variations of the Clark-Y profile with a flat bottom, a smoothly curved top with the thickest part of the profile located at one-third of the profile length from the nose.

The 'Peel' has an extremely unusual profile in that there is a bubble at the back of the wing. This bubble solves the problem many soft-stunters with standard profiles (such as the Clark-Y) have; i.e. that their noses tend to collapse. When a kite is launched, the wind is almost entirely perpendicular to the surface of the kite. As the kite rises higher, its angle of attack in relation to the wind changes constantly. The wind hits the kite at an increasingly smaller angle. If the

kite is flying at the top of the window (or at the very edge of the window) the wind will flow parallel to its surface. As a result the kite will stop moving forward, the pull will decrease and it will lose its balance. A bit of turbulence may cause the nose of the kite to dive to the ground, the rest of the kite collapsing behind it an instant later. There is nothing you can do once this happens. Sparless stunt kites have this problem more often than single-line sparless kites (such as Parafoils) do because the speed with which a stunt kite reaches its zenith is much higher. In other words, the stunt kite tends to 'overshoot' its zenith.

The 'Peel bubble' is said to prevent this from happening. While the kite climbs higher, the bubble is situated in the lee of the wing. Only when the kite flies overhead does the bubble start to catch wind: the air then flows parallel along the profile. The bubble creates resistance and prevents the kite from overshooting its zenith in the wind. It is as though the kite is equipped with an invisible anchor.

As soon as the kite is manoeuvred to the centre of the wind again, the bubble disappears behind the wing amidst a turbulent flow of air and there is, at that moment, no longer any extra drag.

Without such a bubble, the nose of the Sputnik could also collapse. This can easily be fixed by adjusting the trim of the profile by changing the settings of the primary bridle (see page 40).

Finally, there is the S-profile, named after the S-curve of its profile-cord. The cord is the line which indicates the centre of the profile. Flexifoils, Paraflexes and the CS 550 (world's largest kite) all have S-profiles.

In the case of an S-profile, lift not only occurs over the top surface of the wing but also along part of the bottom surface of the profile. The total upward pressure on this profile is, therefore, considerably less than on a standard profile, but without the risk of nose-diving.

The S-profile is often used because the angle of adjustment is self-regulating. We shall not go into details on aerodynamics here, but it boils down to this: the negative lift of the second half of the profile takes over the function of the bridles situated on the trailing half. This is convenient because it simplifies bridling and adjusting significantly. The pull of this negative lift always corresponds to the wind speed and it continuously regulates the proper angle of attack; the tendency for the kite to dive disappears and a one-point bridle becomes sufficient.

The cross-section of a Krypton-S is not a full-fledged S-profile. This has a few advantages: the pull is stronger, yet the two-point bridle is still easy to install and adjust.

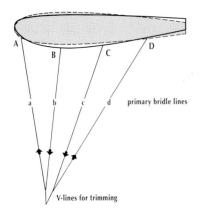

primary bridle lines

V-lines for trimming

3 The shape of the profiles are changed by adjusting the primary bridle lines.

4 The automatic reefing-system reduces the size of the kite by 30 percent when pressure increases.

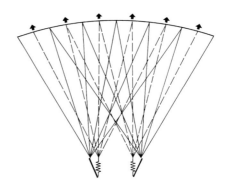

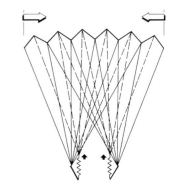

PROFILE TRIM AND BRIDLE

Sputnik 4 has four primary bridle lines for every second or third rib; these support the back of the profiles and give the kite a stronger pull. Adjusting these four bridle lines - and therefore the position of the wing in the wind - must be done very precisely; the bridle lines will either make or break Sputnik 4. For this reason, we have included a list of the exact measurements of all primary bridle lines in the construction plans for Sputnik 4.

The primary bridle has small trim-lines. These lines (each approximately 10 cm long) connect the first and second bridle lines to the third and fourth lines respectively. This means for each profile you have a choice of three adjustment points; however, you will be using the V-line knot at the front for most bridle adjustments. If the Sputnik tends to fly through its zenith and collapse, make line **a** longer and line **b** shorter. If this is not sufficient, then the rearmost V-line can also be adjusted: make line **d** longer and line **c** shorter. By adjusting these lines the bridle is, in fact, not being shifted; rather, the profile is acquiring a round shape. This should prevent the kite from going beyond the wind window. The adjustment line in the centre is used to adjust the appropriate angle of attack without distorting the shape of the profile any further.

The lines connecting the V-lines to the control lines are called secondary bridle lines. The length of the secondary lines controls the typical curved shape of the sparless kite. A correct curvature optimises the pull and manoeuvrability of the kite. With the help of the computer program, the shape of the kite can be changed to a more flat shape or a pronounced parabolic shape. The P.C. will calculate the corresponding set of secondary bridle lines in an instant. For maximum traction you can bridle the kite so that it becomes flatter. Now the wing tips inflate with more difficulty and when you try to make small loops the

kite will tend to collapse. Maximum manoeuvrability is reached with a deep curve in the wing at the same time reducing the pull of the kite.

The spacing of the secondary bridle line connections onto the arch have been set so as to prevent, as much as possible, the shape of the kite from distorting during manoeuvres. This is why the bridle lines in the middle of the arch are so close together and the lines at the edges so far apart.

BRIDLE ATTACHMENT

There was no satisfactory solution to the problem of connecting the primary bridle to the kite. We used keels to distribute the pull on our Sputniks 1 and 2 (Cf. *Stunt Kites - To Make and Fly*). But keels cause a lot of resistance and take a lot of time to assemble.

We finally found the solution in the internals of a 'Peel'. On each rib with a set of primary bridle lines, a line is stitched in a zig-zag fashion. When you finish the kite, all you have to do is take a needle and prick the primary bridle lines through the bottom skin, go around the reinforcement line and thread the line through the skin again. There you make a bridle-hitch (Cf. Appendix on 'Knots'). The V-shaped lines distribute the pull over the entire profile, preventing creases from forming; you will not notice any distortions on the outside. Wonderful!

THE AUTOMATIC REEFING SYSTEM

A serious buggy rider will have several kites at hand when he sets out. For example, a large Speedwing for 7 Beaufort winds, a 3 m² Sputnik for 5 Beaufort winds and an 8 m² for 3 Beaufort winds. But which kite should he use for 4 Beaufort winds? A 3 m² will be too small to gain any speed, especially upwind. Yet an 8 m² will pull him out of the buggy.

Lynn found the answer to this by adding elastic shock-cords to the secondary bridle lines. When the power of the 'Peel' exceeds a certain point, these shock-cords (adjustable by varying the length, thickness and number of lines) stretch, causing the top of the kite to bulge out and the kite to compress like an accordion, reducing the surface area of the kite. The disadvantage of this invention is that because the shape of the kite becomes distorted as a result of this, it will become less efficient, and therefore slower. Moreover, the kite will not fly well at the edges of the wind window.

If the wind conditions are stable, you can reach optimum speeds with a kite of the right proportions without an automatic reefing system. However, when winds are turbulent or not very reliable, the reefing system is a good option.

We discovered a 'neater' solution where the primary bridle lines rather than the secondary ones are regulated. The foremost two primary lines consist of Dyneema/Spectra line, the rearmost two of Dacron. As you know, Dacron stretches much more than Dyneema does. As the pressure on the kite increases, the back of the kite will push up. The kite's angle of attack is reduced and the pull of the kite will decrease without losing efficiency; it will even improve in efficiency and reach a higher angle of flight.

NUMBER OF RIBS

The usual shape of the profile of a kite differs from the shape of the ribs which are stitched into the kite - this is because the fabric of the cells billows out. The difference between the two is actually considerable, and this needs to be taken into account when designing the kite. If you were to suddenly double the number of the ribs in a Sputnik (74 instead of 37), the shape of the average profile will become thinner. As a result, the Sputnik would become too thin and too weak. You can add or reduce the number of ribs in the kite, but then you will have to change their shape in order to create the 'same' kite. Selecting the quantity of ribs is particularly important when enlarging or shrinking the design - the number of ribs must then be adapted in order to retain the correct shape of the kite. If we take a design which is X times larger, as a rule of thumb the distance between the profiles will increase by the square root of X. The number which comes out of this formula should, of course, be rounded off so that you come out with a 'whole' number of cells with an 'appropriate' number of profiles equipped with bridle attachments. In the designs you will find varying bridle attachments per 2 or 3 cells.

GAUZE

As can be seen in Figure 1 (page 38), most of the lift occurs at the nose of the wing. This is why we have chosen gauze for the opening where the air flows in. Thus the shape of the nose of the kite distorts as little as possible. You can use large-meshed gauze or so-called technical gauze fabric sold in kite stores.

Regarding the location of the strip of gauze, an additional point: we have indicated exactly where the gauze should come in our construction plans and computer program; however, generally speaking, the gauze should be as narrow as possible and should be located at the pressure point, that is to say, the point where the wind pushes against the nose of the kite at right angles (Cf. Figure 1: the area with the highest pressure is indicated just under the nose of the profile where the gauze should be located). If the gauze is misplaced, the wings will have difficulty inflating or will not inflate at all.

ASPECT RATIO

The ratio of the wingspan to the average chord (= profile length) of the kite is called the Aspect Ratio (A.R.). In aerodynamic terms: A.R. = B/C.

B is the wingspan of the kite, C the average chord. In a high A.R., the wingspan of a kite is wide and the chord not deep, in a low A.R. short and deep respectively. A square kite, for example, has an A.R. of 1.

Theoretically, a high A.R. wing is more efficient than one with a low A.R. But the higher the A.R., the more the wing tends to distort into the shape of a banana; the tips lag behind the centre of the kite. This tendency occurs partly because of the thickness and the shape of the profile (see p. 38, 'The Profile').

The compromise is somewhere between an A.R. of 3 and 4.5. The Flexifoil has an A.R. of 3, Sputnik 4 an A.R. of approximately 4.0 and some of our experimental models are 4.5 times wide as their depth. Tapering models require a bit of calculating in order to find out what the average chord is. The alternative A.R. formula: A.R. = B²/S comes in handy then. S is the surface area of the kite.

The computer program allows you to play around with the A.R. of your Sputnik.

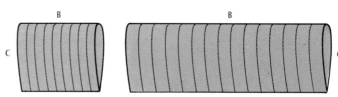

10 KITE POWER

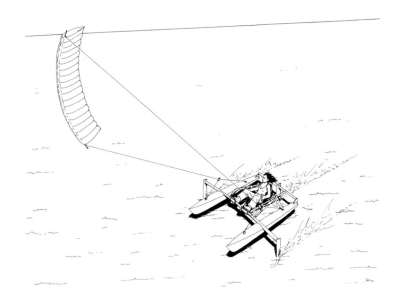

1 *Peter Lynn on his buggy-boat. The hull in the front functions as a rudder.*

Stunt kites provide controllable power. The pilot determines the direction of the power created by the kite and, in the case of quad-line kites, even determines the amount of power generated. In the chapter 'So, What's New?' we briefly dealt with stunt kites as a power source for skis, skeelers, buggies and boats. Let us continue our story.

Not long after the 'new-style' stunt kite was introduced (in the mid-seventies), kite flyers began to use the dormant powers of this sophisticated toy for new areas. The Englishman Ian Day, for example, used a train of 15 large Flexifoils to pull a modified Tornado catamaran at extremely high speeds. Between 1982 and 1988, Day held the world record for speed sailing in the C-class (sail surface area between 21.8 and 27.9 m²): 25.5 knots (47.2 km/h) was the highest speed ever recorded.

In the years following, kite flyers started doing even crazier things with their 'eco-engines': racing along at high speeds while wearing anything from slippery gym shoes to skates, skeelers, sand-skis, snow-skis, grass-skis (a kind of mini Caterpillar) and water-skis. The last technique, in particular, should be taken seriously. After four years of experimenting, the Roeslers, a father and son team from San Diego, managed to build a reliable flying system. Using a couple of standard water-skis, a modified Banshee stunt kite (7 m wingspan,

single-piece curved leading edge), an aluminum control bar and a pulley on the bar for winding the line in case the kite crashed into the water, they created the new sport of kite water-skiing. Cory, the son, repeatedly beat the fastest windsurfers - the highest speed so far is 34 knots. According to Cory, however, it is only a matter of time before he hits 50 knots (thereby breaking a new world record for speed-sailing).

Although we have never tried it ourselves, another sport from Germany has appeared on the scene. It is a cross between stunt kite flying and 'parasailing' (manned parachutes pulled behind boats or cars). Wolfgang Beringer from Lorch produces extremely large parawings (maximum size 25 m²). A Parawing is a square-shaped, sparless wing with three rows of keels running along its wingspan. Bridle lines connect the keels to a sturdy control bar. The uppermost bundle of bridle lines come together at one end of the bar, the middle row is connected to its centre and the lowermost row converges at the other end of the bar. By turning the control bar, the pilot can directly change the parawing's flight direction and angle of attack. The control bar is connected by a line to a harness around the pilot's waist. The whole contraption looks like a 'tamed'

2 Controling a parawing. By rotating the control bar the position of the kite changes.

3 The buggy-boat is light, it can be dismantled and is easy to sail. Here a prototype (with winged-keels for easy planing).

4 Details of the ice-buggy. The skates, sharp as razor blades, become blunt quickly due to high speeds.

parachute. The disadvantage of this system is that, unlike a kite, a Parawing cannot 'create wind by itself' - the reason Parawings have to be much larger than kites in order to create the same amount of power. The Reinhold and Hubert Messner brothers (the former a famous mountain climber) skied over Greenland in 1993 with the help of Parawings. They covered 2,200 kilometres, or roughly 60 kilometres a day, in 35 days.

Without kites they probably would have covered no more than 30 kilometres a day.

For 'normal' people like you and us, stunt kites can be used, in particular, to pull boats and buggies. You can read about the latter in chapter 11, *Buggying*, and in Appendix III, *Buggy*. Here we provide you with information on 'kite-sailing', i.e. sailing with the help of kites.

There are five good reasons why you should consider kite-sailing. Firstly, from a kite flyer's or buggy-rider's viewpoint the less space there is for racing over a beach with a power-kite, the more attractive lakes and oceans become. If your flying site is shrinking, switch to water.

Secondly, from a sailor's viewpoint winds are more stable and stronger 30 or 50 metres above the water than immediately above it. Kites, therefore, encounter much 'better' winds than sails. Thirdly, kites tend not to capsize boats. Sails on boats are attached to a mast located right on the deck so that with a strong wind boats can capsize. If anything, a kite would pull a boat out of the water rather than capsize it.

Fourthly, by manoeuvring the kite from one side to the other, the pilot can increase its speed. The kite will 'associate' this speed with increasing wind (so-called 'Apparent Wind') and start pulling harder. In theory, therefore, a kite is much more efficient per square metre than a sail.

Finally, there is the advantage of a kite-boat's design. It can be built much lighter than a sailing boat because it does not need a mast or a supporting construction.

So why do sailing boats still exist? Mainly for practical reasons - imagine a lake or river packed with kite-sailors all getting their lines tangled up! Sailing boats take up less space in the sky (a practical point to consider on small lakes). Kite-boats also have several more serious disadvantages. For instance, it is difficult for a navigator to launch a kite-boat when his/her hands are literally full with a kite. Also, should the kite crash into the water the flyer has to retrieve the kite and return it to land to dry before being able to relaunch it.

But perhaps the strongest argument in favour of the sailing boat versus the kite-boat is purely a psychological one. Not only have sailing boats existed for centuries, they have always been taken extremely seriously. Kite-boats, on the other hand, are a recent invention and tend to attract the more eccentric types of flyers.

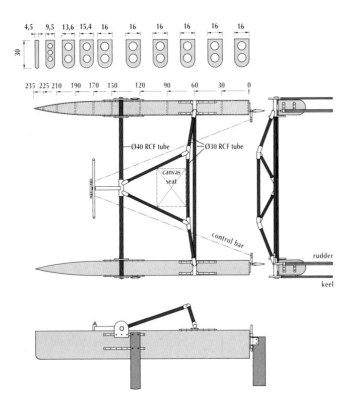

5 *This catamaran is constructed out of wood, carbon and steel tubes, and is used for sailing on lakes.*

BUGGY-BOAT

The man who has probably spent the most time and energy experimenting with kites on water is, once again, Peter Lynn. More than 60 prototype kite-boats have sailed on the cold waters of Lake Clearwater in New Zealand before Lynn came up with the buggy-boat, now available commercially. The wheels of the buggy are simply replaced by three identical glass-fibre hulls, thereby creating a compact but stable trimaran. As far as development is concerned, the cycle is now complete. The original buggy, such as the one currently on the market, was actually a modification of a trimaran during an older experiment - at the time the hulls were replaced by wheels.

This symmetrical trimaran is well-known for its high stability - it can cope extremely well with high waves. During the fifties and sixties, coastal rescue teams at Scheveningen, on the Dutch North Sea coast, used similar vessels - but with oars - to rescue people from drowning.

The success of the trimaran has not yet been attributed to its speed. In fact, the speed of a windsurfer can only be equalled if the trimaran is on a downwind course. On an upwind one a windsurfer sails twice as fast as the trimaran. The buggy-boat is actually a multi-purpose craft: when the beaches get crowded in summer you can easily switch to kite-sailing and, thanks to the three small hulls, the boat is easy to transport and store.

The disappointing speed of the 'water-buggy' is due to three main reasons. Firstly, the combination of the three hulls creates extreme resistance. Secondly, the surface area of a kite is too limited: the power necessary to generate high speeds would also pull the pilot out of his boat. Thirdly, the effectiveness of a kite is far inferior to that of a modern sail. Windsurfers can sail much higher into the wind, even when their sails have the same surface area as a kite. A kite reaches a good Lift/Area Ratio only when it has gained speed (when it performs loops or figures of eight) and this is only possible in diagonally downwind courses.

While searching for a faster alternative to the buggy-boat, we did some experimenting ourselves. We provide drawings of a small single-person catamaran we designed for those who want to reach high speeds on smooth water. The boat does sail fast and it also has a few imperfections, especially concerning navigation. The two slender hulls tend to go in a straight line, like a train on a railway track, though once it gains momentum the catamaran has no problem changing course. At lower speeds, however, this becomes more difficult. When tacking upwind, it is difficult to make the necessary tight turns.

We are still pondering how to connect a kite to the flyer and to the boat. It is of course much safer for a flyer not to be secured to a boat and to have the kite in his/her own hands. The disadvantage is that either the kite must be small (so the flyer cannot be pulled out of the craft) or the size of the boat is limited (such as the trimaran, our catamaran, or ultimately, water-skis).

On a larger and heavier vessel with a crew of several people, the kite would have to be secured to the vessel through some sort of ingenious control system because the power of the kite(s) can easily amount to hundreds of kilograms. But attaching a kite either to the flyer or the vessel can lead to dangerous results as the following two incidents show.

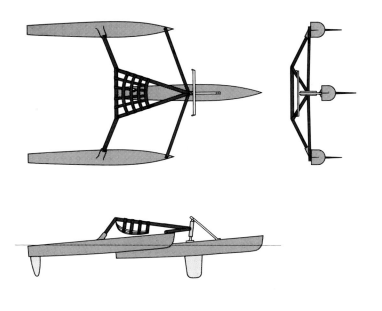

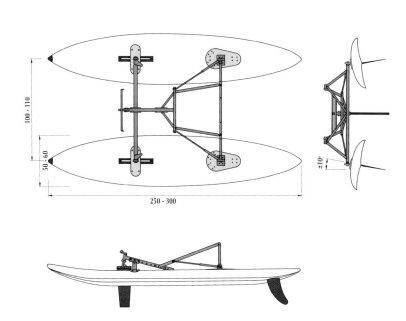

6 *Buggy-boat: comfortable and safe.*

The first incident involved someone flying an extremely stable kite attached to a boat. The flyer fell overboard after making a wrong manoeuvre with his kite. The kite, which had no intention of crashing into the sea, flew off at breakneck speed with the boat dangling from its lines, leaving the flyer to swim back to shore. Hours later, he finally found his vessel and kite *several kilometres inland* where the boat had come to a halt after crashing into a tree. The kite was still airborne.

The other incident involved the famous 'Jacob's Ladder', the above mentioned Tornado catamaran pulled by a train of Flexifoils. The stack of kites were attached to the hulls, a strong gust of wind suddenly caused the ladder of kites to pull both the boat and its two navigators into the air. The Tornado hung vertically in the sky for a while, the sailors fell out of the boat and, some distance downwind, it eventually crashed.

So what else can you do? Connect the kite to your own body and secure yourself to the vessel? You will certainly not lose the kite or your boat this way, but it surely is the quickest way to drown.

Let us suppose you or we come up with an extremely fast kite-boat. Imagine all the problems have been solved: the kite(s) maintain a strong pull (even if the boat is sailing fast), the navigator is not flung out of the boat, the boat is easy to

7 *The 'surfboard-boat' designed by Stef Tours: made out of two 'semi-sinkers' and a four-wheel buggy frame. The rudder is located in the front, making the boat very manoeuvrable.*

steer, etc. There is only one more question we must ask ourselves. Where do we attempt to break the world record for speed sailing (85.5 km/h) or speed surfing (83.96 km/h)? The answer: Saintes Maries de la Mer, Camarque, in the South of France. Here a canal was dug behind a beach especially for speed-trials. The canal, known as the 'French Trench', is 1,300 metres long, 20 metres wide and 1.20 metres deep. Flying conditions are ideal: undisturbed winds blow straight from the Mediterranean and there are hardly any waves.

Once there the only thing you have to do is to wait for strong winds (8 - 9 Beaufort) from the right direction (under a 120° angle in relation to the canal) and then, just go for it!

Imagine your kite flying stably in the power zone, your boat shooting forward and soon cruising on the water at 100 km/h... it is too bad the French Trench ends so abruptly. Within 45 seconds you are forced to end your speed-run by crashing onto land at the far end!

11 BUGGYING

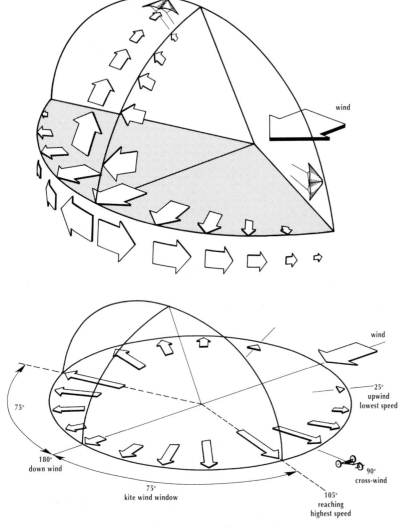

wind

wind

25°
upwind
lowest speed

75°

180°
down wind

75°
kite wind window

105°
reaching
highest speed

90°
cross-wind

1 The wind range of a kite. The strongest pull is found in the centre of the wind window.

2 The wind range of a buggy. The buggy reaches its highest speed at approximately 100 - 120 degrees from the wind (long arrows).

Looking back, it is obvious why the sport of buggying was born. Power kites with the capacity to drag along adults at great speed became available, we now have the necessary extremely thin, virtually unbreakable lines and, of course, there was always the example of George Pocock. Around 1826, Pocock used manoeuvrable arch-top kites to pull carriages around the English countryside. These kites resembled Eddy kites except that they had arched heads. In his book *A Treatise of the Aeropleustic Art*, published in 1851, Pocock claimed it was possible for a lightweight carriage (a so-called char-volant), carrying four or five passengers, to be pulled by a kite at speeds of 30 km/h. Pocock flew a stack of several kites, manoeuvring them with four lines so he could fly in all directions. Although we are somewhat sceptical about this story (a carriage without rubber tires, carrying five passengers, going as fast as 30 km/h up and down the muddy, hilly English countryside?), Pocock's invention remains, nevertheless, an undisputed fact. He was the first man to apply the concept of a buggy.

During the century and a half between then and now, there have been many eccentrics who have experimented with the traction of carts and boats induced by kites, but it is Peter Lynn from New Zealand who perfected the sport of buggying as we know it today. The Lynn-buggy is a three-wheeled cart, completely detachable, made of stainless-steel tubing. Weighing only about eight kilograms, transporting it is no problem.

The buggy rider sits between the two rear wheels and steers the front wheel with the feet. The wheels are small so that the elbows of the rider do not hit the tires.

In a way buggying resembles the sport of ice-sailing. In both sports it is possible to go faster than the speed of wind and reach top speeds of about 100 km/h. (As far as ice-sailing is concerned, we refer to the standard type such as the *DN*. The world ice-sailing record has been set at an unbelievable 233.6 km/h). Obviously a fall occurring during either sport can have serious consequences, but more about that later.

In order to explain the workings of buggy-riding we need to go over a few simple, theoretical points. If you are an experienced windsurfer or sailor, you will have a definite advantage over others.

The kite must be regarded as a 'sail' at a distance. However, there is at least one difference between buggying and sailing in that the angle of a kite in relation to the wind cannot be controlled as is the case with a sail. What is controllable is the location of the kite as it flies, meaning its direction and (indirectly) the traction of the lines on the kite which, in turn, pull the buggy.

Figure 1 is a diagram representing a kite's wind window. The arrows on the surface in Figure 2 indicate the various directions a buggy can take; the length of the arrows represent the relative speed for each direction. As you will see, the buggy (on a hard surface) has a wider range than a kite does. This is illustrated in Figures 2 and 3. Say you need a forward force of 10 kg to get the buggy going (we know we should say 100 Newton, but we do not want to sound too formal). This corresponds to more than 14 kg at 45°, 20 kg at 60° and 58 kg at 80°. In theory, the buggy can ride with a line-angle between 0 and 89.9°, though in practice this is very much limited because of the increase in the power required. In strong winds and soft sand conditions the limit lies at approximately 45°, while in ideal, hard-packed sand conditions at approximately 80°.

A kite can fly 75° to the left and right respectively. This applies to kites with a relatively good Lift Drag ratio

of approximately 4:1 (see page 55). Take another look at Figure 2. You will notice that the buggy has a maximum heading of 25° into the wind as the following shows: Heading = buggy drag angle + kite drag angle; Heading = (90°-80°) + (90°-75°); Heading = 10° + 15° = 25°.

The kite pulls least at the edges of the wind window; traction comes at an almost right angle to the buggy, which is very inefficient. In other words, the speed in this heading is extremely low; on soft surfaces the maximum angle into the wind drastically decreases. Under ideal circumstances you can reach 25°, in most cases up to 45°, and on soft sands 90° is the maximum, which is no more than a half-wind course.

So it is clear that the buggy-kite combination does work. However, as soon as

a buggy begins to move there is a problem: the phenomenon of Apparent Wind. If you stand in a windless gym and sprint at 20 km/h you feel a 20 km/h head-wind. This so-called 'Apparent Wind' is created by your own movement. If you do the same sprint outside with 20 km/h tail winds you do not feel any wind at all. But if you run into 20 km/h headwinds, you suddenly feel 40 km/h head-winds. If the same 20 km/h wind is at a right angle to your running course, you feel 28 km/h winds at a 45° diagonal angle (Cf. Vectors in Figure 6). If you run faster, you feel the side winds almost directly in your face. This is what makes buggying such fun. No matter which course you ride in relation to the (true) wind, the wind increasingly feels as though it is coming from the front as the speed of the buggy increases. The kite naturally feels this too, so the speed of the

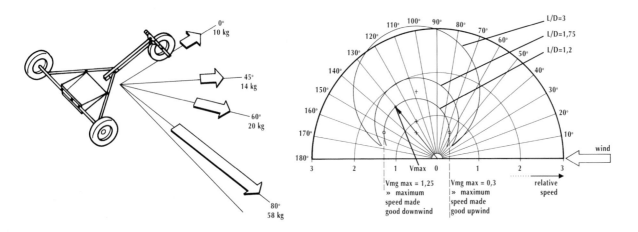

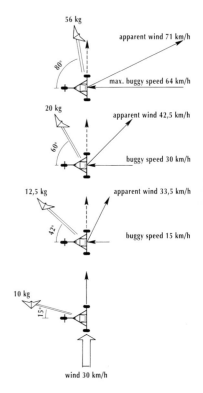

3 The diagonal pull on the buggy increases considerably when the kite flies almost perpendicular to the buggy course.

4 The polar curves indicate the fastest speeds attainable on various courses.

5 The buggy on a cross-wind course. The higher the speed, the stronger the Apparent Wind from the front.

7 During a jib the buggy rider skids sideways.

6 The vectors show how Apparent Wind originates.

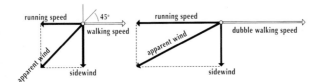

buggy increases until the Apparent Wind comes too strongly from the front. In the above example that would be a 25° angle.

Except on a direct downwind course, all courses eventually become upwind courses in relation to the Apparent Wind. After acceleration of both kite and buggy, the kite comes to rest at approximately 80° from the buggy course and remains flying there at the same speed as the buggy. The kite is situated at the edge of its wind window and, therefore, 105° from the Apparent Wind. Assuming the surface is hard, the Apparent Wind is 25° in relation to the buggy course. Take a look at Figure 5: a buggy accelerates to its maximum speed on a reaching (crosswind) course in four stages. Eventually, it reaches an Apparent Wind speed 2.4 times the true wind speed and the buggy speed 2.1 times the wind speed. The highest buggy speed of 2.3 times the wind speed is possible on

courses between 100° and 110° from the wind. It is interesting to watch buggies go downwind faster than the wind itself at 120° to 140° from the wind. By tacking downwind you can in fact catch up with the wind!

The performance of a buggy depends largely on the L/D ratio of the kite as well as the rolling resistance of the buggy tires. By measuring the minimum angle at which you can point into the wind, you can determine the L/D ratio of the kite-buggy combination. On hard-packed sand, a buggy/Sputnik combination can sometimes reach about 35°; L/D = 1/tan35° = 1.6. This means the combination can reach 1.6 times the wind speed. Figure 4 gives a number of polar curves for various L/D ratios of the buggy and kite. You can easily see which buggy speeds can be reached on various courses in relation to the wind speed.

With the L/D ratio of 1.6, the Vmg-max (Velocity Made Good) is larger than 1.

It follows, then, that you should just be able to catch up with a little balloon being carried off by the wind. All the above-mentioned figures have been tested and confirmed with the help of wind-metres and speedometers on the wide beaches of the Dutch island of Vlieland. The only thing we have not tried is the challenge of overtaking a gliding balloon - an interesting idea we hope to put into effect one day during a buggy event!

After reading the above, you may conclude that it is easy for a buggy to reach fantastic speeds, but in reality such speeds are much harder to attain than you think. If you sit on a buggy with the kite parked at the edge of the wind window, waiting for your buggy to pick up speed, nothing much will happen. You first need to move the kite. In the centre of the wind a kite flies up to four times faster than the speed of the wind - 100 km/h in 4 to 5 Beaufort winds. The power is 16 times stronger than that of a similar size stationary kite. A quick calculation tells you that if a Sputnik in a stable position above your head has a traction of, for example, 10 kg, this becomes 160 kg in a power dive. Wonderful in terms of initial buggy acceleration...but after that?

On your first try you soon discover that riding directly downwind does not work. The lines slacken, the kite is no longer controllable and can eventually crash. Start by riding across from the wind as much as possible, hold the kite at least 10° to 15° in front of the imaginary line through the rear axle of the buggy and keep up the flying-speed of the kite by continuously dipping it into and out of its power zone. Dips are always made into the direction you are buggying. You will notice that as your speed increases the kite no longer has to move as much to maintain traction. The Apparent Wind does the job while you point the kite's nose in the same direction as the buggy's course. Once you have reached this stage, buggying becomes truly enjoyable. It is then time to try luffing and bearing away.

Luffing means changing to a more upwind course. The buggy's speed immediately drops because the kite pulls it more from the side. In order to gain traction and also prevent the kite from flying out of the wind window, once again manoeuvre the kite up and down in a dipping motion. Instead of a reaching (crosswind) course, you now follow an upwind course and gain ground in relation to this wind. You can go upwind as far as the buggy allows you to; when the buggy stops moving, the limit has been reached. Turn downwind on time or you will have to step out of the buggy to reposition it in the right direction.

Bearing away means changing to a more downwind course. The speed of the buggy increases and reaches its maximum on downwind courses at about 110° from the true wind. If you 'bear away' any further, the pressure of the kite decreases - the trick is to keep the kite moving by making loops or figure-eights.

Stopping the buggy is accomplished by turning upwind, while at the same time placing the kite high above the head.

Tacking is a zigzag course, necessary when you go upwind. The trick here is to find the exact course that allows you to gain ground in the most efficient way. Tacking by using courses close to the wind means less speed but also less turning points. Aiming for higher speeds and a less direct course means you have to make more turns and therefore lose more ground. To compensate for this you need to attain higher speeds.

Going About: Obviously you need to change direction at some point, but it is not possible to ride the buggy directly up- or downwind. However, you need to go through either direction in order to complete a turn. You can reverse direction efficiently by doing the following: you are buggying at a constant speed on a reaching (crosswind) course with the kite to your right, the wind to your left. Manoeuvre the kite upwards, making sure you keep your centre of gravity low by leaning backwards in your seat. In one quick motion steer the buggy to the right. The buggy will make a short turn downwind - at that moment direct the kite into the centre of the wind window. Without decreasing speed too much, you can now buggy to the other end. In sailing terms this is called a 'jib'. Short turns are important; if you are overly cautious and take a wide turn, you wind up riding downwind and the chances of your kite falling out of the sky greatly increase.

Turning upwind (going about) is possible; there are first-rate buggyers who certainly can do it. But they are experts who can also buggy in reverse, pop two-wheelers and make 360° spins. Neither you nor we have reached that stage yet.

First try to master the buggy at high speeds. It is important to be prepared for emergencies (for example, an unleashed dog appearing out of the blue in front of you), so practice stopping at high speeds by quickly turning the buggy into the wind - even if it means skidding sideways - until the buggy comes to a standstill.

Something else is bound to happen one day - you will topple out of the buggy. This happens most frequently during an uncontrolled manoeuvre or when your feet accidentally slip off the steering bars (e.g. due to a pot-hole). The steering bars have vertical tubes protruding from the ends against which the feet can be placed. Toe clips (such as used by bicycle racers) are not recommended because these can cause broken ankles, but it does help to cover the steering bars with some kind of rough material. Try sandpaper, bicycle handlebar foam or some other material. However, even such accessories may not prevent you from losing contact with the steering bars. The buggy then tumbles over its front wheel and at

8 Do not panic - an intentional wheely.

speeds of 25 to 75 km/h you get thrown out of the buggy and land on hard-packed sand. Fortunately the fall occurs only from a height of ten centimetres! Nevertheless the injuries may be considerable, painful and annoying. Until now we have only experienced bruises and lacerations on our hips and elbows, but we can assure you that the consequences can be much worse.

A sensible buggier - and you will certainly become one after a few nasty falls - wears strong shoes, long pants, a shirt with long sleeves and a secure-fitting helmet (we prefer bicycle or canoe helmets because they are light and water-resistant).

You can prevent many initial mishaps by starting with smaller kites. A Speedwing - such as the one in this book - is a good kite to practice with in medium and strong winds. Interestingly enough, the difference in buggy speed by using a Speedwing instead of a much larger 'Foil' type kite is actually quite small. One afternoon we timed a Speedwing-powered buggy at 35 km/h and using a 2.5m² Peel we clocked 42 km/h: the Peel was 250 per cent larger than the Speedwing yet only 25 per cent faster.

On the other hand smaller kites can in some cases be even faster. Sometimes when flying a large kite in certain wind conditions you are confronted with problems as soon as the buggy increases its speed. The increase in Apparent Wind causes the pressure on a kite to increase. This kite traction is almost perpendicular to the buggy's riding direction. Tires only offer resistance to side-forces up to a point; beyond that they skid sideways or 'drift'. To compensate for this diversion from the original course, the rider should luff the buggy. The rear wheels will sway to one side as the front wheel is steered into the opposite direction; the combined motion prevents the buggy from reaching high speeds. In this case a slightly smaller kite is the thing to use: the wheels no longer lose their grip, the buggy wheels stay on track and there is no need for steering-corrections. Upon reaching higher speeds you will no doubt confront sideways skidding at some point. The best way to handle this is by leaning forward in the buggy and holding the kite lines very low so that the forces are balanced between the front and rear wheels. The rider with this kind of technique will no doubt win the race.

What race? Of course! Buggy-racing is still a young sport and as yet there are no official race regulations. However, what has recently become popular and spectacular to watch in kite festivals is pursuit-racing on reaching (crosswind) courses. The object of the race is to pursue and pass the opponent as fast as possible. Two small flagpoles for turning points are set 100 to 200 metres apart, in a line perpendicular to the wind direction. The participants start from opposite ends of the

racing track. With consistently high speeds (upwind tacking is not necessary) and sand-spraying turns, it is great fun to watch such a race. Moreover, spectators have a very clear view of what is going on during the race. Few rules are necessary. In fact even simple rules, for example the rule that opponents must pass each other on the right side to avoid collision do not always work because kites and lines get in the way.

Besides speed, tactics also play an important role in this sport. The shortest way from A to B is not necessarily the fastest. After reversing directions, it is better to accelerate quickly by going slightly downwind, then ride a reaching course to a point which is slightly downwind from Flag B where, at the last minute, you once again turn up into the wind. By doing so you lose some speed in order to make the quick but safe turn. You can also ride 'defensively'. If your opponent is better and faster than you are, get in his way by starting at an upwind course with your kite flying as low as possible above the beach. He is then forced to choose an inefficient course or a *sur-place* (as in bicycle sprint-racing) may take place with lines crossed.

The surface of the beach between the turning points is never consistent. Try avoiding soft areas. If this is not possible, the quickest solution is to power through it on a more downwind course so that you can luff back upwind after reaching harder ground.

Because buggies, like sailing boats, can go anywhere, other race tracks -

9 *It takes a while to find one's bearings, but then it is a fantastic experience: a kilometres-wide dry lake in the Southwest of North America.*

10 *During a buggy race chaos can ensue around the downwind flagpole.*

such as a three-point course - are possible. Due to the spacious lay-out of the course, the number of riders wishing to participate in the race is unlimited. The track is divided in three 'tacks'. The upwind and reaching tacks are easy to buggy - anyone can follow them. The difference between being a champion or a loser lies in how one tackles the downwind tack.

The shortest way to reach the downwind buoy is also the slowest one (see above). The thing to do is to tack: a 150° downwind tack over to one side, jib, then tack over to the other side, jib, etc. If a rider tries to gain speed the normal way (vertical eights, manoeuvring the kite slowly towards the ground) it takes too long for the buggy to pick up speed. What the rider should do is this. If the buggy is tacking from left to right, then the kite has to fly exactly in the opposite direction, from right to left. When the kite threatens to fly too far *behind* the rider, he must shift the kite and buggy at the same time: a jib. While the buggy is now riding with the wind from right to left, the kite is flying from left to right. The clever thing about this steering method is that the kite is 'fooled' into feeling the wind is constantly coming from the front, so it reacts by exerting a consistent pulling force. Timing is crucial: if the rider does it right, the kite and buggy cross each other in the centre of their respective flying and riding courses. In such a situation, speeds increase so much that the rider eventually feels the wind blowing straight into the face on the downwind stretch!

11 Buggies awaiting the start signal.

Then comes the most difficult turn: a full-speed jib at the buoy at the most downwind location. The rider reduces his speed a little (by placing the kite slightly behind him) and makes a full turn with all the confidence he possesses. It takes practice!

Rules for buggy racing are simple: a) the one who lags a lap behind is out; b) if your kite crashes you must relaunch it yourself and c) the last one left on the track is the winner.

There are several kite models suitable for buggying. The large Peel (5 and 7.5 m²) and our 5 m² or 10 m² Sputnik 4 are the best for light and medium winds. In stronger winds the Speedwing is a good option. Two Speedwings stacked together are sometimes not only faster than a Sputnik, but also easier to control when buggying. Our experience with other types of kites is not that positive - most have the disadvantage of being unable to pull enough at the edges of the wind window, exactly the spot where a kite flies most of the time during buggying.

The easiest way to learn buggying is to practice with a small kite on a hard-packed sand beach devoid of people and dogs, in medium to strong onshore winds (about 4 - 5 Beaufort winds). Bear in mind that you will be completely covered with sand, salt and water by the end of a practice session.

An afternoon of buggying will make you look like some miserable mud-wrestler. In summer we recommend you wear a 'wet-suit', in winter a 'dry-suit' or water-tight sailing outfit that covers your body from top to toe. We also use close-fitting ski goggles to protect our eyes.

Stash away in a safe place such items as house keys, wallets and pocket knives before buggying.

And finally, where to buggy? Good question. In theory you can buggy just about anywhere where there is open space, a hard surface, few or no trees, and where no one else is around. A flat meadow on top of a hill would be great, but an island off Europe-coast with kilometres of hard-packed beaches or a dry lake in the American desert are ideal locations. However, most of us have to make do with our local surroundings - in our case, the beaches of the North Sea coast. However, these beaches can only be used during low tide, in steady northwesterly winds, and only when the beaches are free of strollers and dogs. In summer this means we can only go buggying early in the morning before holidaymakers arrive, or later in the evening when they have gone. If you know of a good location let us know (and do not tell anyone else!).

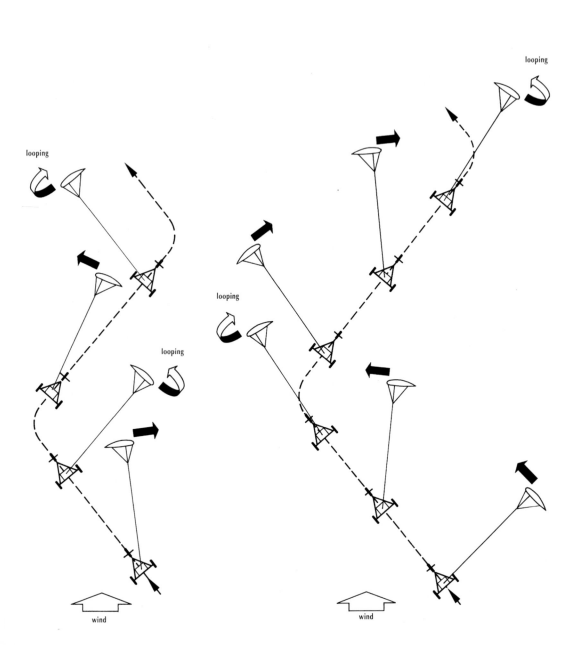

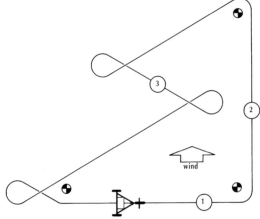

13 A buggy-race on a triangular course.

12 Crossing downwind. Left: the radical technique used on a downwind stretch (on a narrow beach, for example). Right: the technique used where there is ample space.

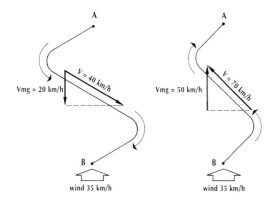

14 *Velocity Made Good: who can reach the buoy first?*

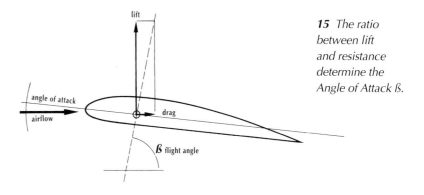

15 *The ratio between lift and resistance determine the Angle of Attack ß.*

Vmg

Vmg stands for Velocity Made Good. Say you want to go from point A against the wind to point B in 35 km/h winds, 10 km away. In order to reach B it is necessary to tack upwind. If that occurs at tacks of 60° toward the wind, you cover a distance of 20 kilometres (10/cos60°). At a speed of 40 km/h it takes 30 minutes to get to B. The Vmg is then: 10 km in 30 min. = 20 km/h.

The same is true for the return ride from B to A in tail winds. Again, you go faster by tacking downwind than when you head in a straight line.

On a course of 135°, for example, the speeds will be higher, perhaps 70 km/h, the distance that you have to cover 10/cos135°=14 km. It will take 0.2 hours to return to A; the Vmg is then 10/0.2 = 50 km/h. This is faster than the wind blowing from B to A! The arrow Vmg-max in the pole-diagram of Figure 5 indicates the direction one must ride in order to attain the highest possible Vmg.

RELATIVE SPEED

It is often more useful to use the term *relative speed* rather than buggy speed: how fast the buggy goes in relation to the wind. In the above example - 70 km/h in 35 km/h winds - the relative speed is 2. The Vmg relative is 50/35= 1.43. In a relative speed of 1 the buggy's speed is equal to the speed of the wind. In the pole-diagram of Figure 5 we refer to relative speed.

L/D

L/D stands for Lift/Drag: the ratio of, in this case, the force of the vertical lift and the force of the horizontal drag of a kite. This term is often used to indicate the efficiency of aerodynamic objects. If a kite in flight has a drag of, for example, 10 kg while it has the power to lift 50 kg, then the L/D = 50/10 = 5 (the weight of the kite itself has been neglected here). This also determines the maximum angle of the kite (Cf. Figure 15). When a kite is above your head, the line-angle is: ß = arctan L/D. And vice versa: by measuring the maximum angle the kite can reach in stable winds we can also determine what the L/D of the kite is: L/D = tan ß (at that particular wind speed).

HOW TO SURVIVE BUGGYING

1 Wear protective clothing: strong shoes or boots, long pants, upper clothing with long sleeves, ski goggles, *helmet*.
2 If there are other people on the site, give them a wide berth.
3 Check your equipment (buggy, lines, clothes, kite) regularly.
4 Do not use a harness unless you use automatic quick-release handles.
5 Stay clear of electricity wires.
6 Make sure you are in good physical condition. People who are fit suffer fewer injuries in a crash.
7 Do not buggy when it is too crowded on the buggy course.
8 Get supplementary third-party liability insurance.

12 THE COLLECTION

Perhaps you are about to close this book and design a kite yourself. Good idea! But if you would like to make a kite with the help of construction plans just one last time, here is some general information regarding the eight new designs featured in this book:

ZIPP

Have you ever tried teaching a beginner how to fly a stunt kite and found the experience a total flop? Usually the problem lies with the kite, not the beginner - a Trillby or a Shuttle is too lethargic, a Flexifoil is always launched upside down, a Speedwing is too skittish, a Spin-off too fragile and a Sputnik is almost impossible to repair if a profile gets torn in the learning process. How we ever managed to learn kite flying ourselves seems a miracle!

The solution is the Zipp. The frame of the Zipp consists of 4 mm solid carbon fibre rods, making it almost indestructible. Because of the large camber in the nose, the kite is easy to launch even in light winds (e.g. 2 Beaufort winds). Moreover, because it is small the Zipp does not pull hard even in 6 Beaufort winds, it hardly makes any noise, is able to reach respectable speeds and can make quick, but not too radical, turns. We know of at least one group of flyers who use the Zipp for team flying in strong winds.

The Zipp weighs 105 grams and has a surface area of 0.37 m² (284 gr/m²). As well as for the basic Zipp, measurements for two larger versions - the Medium Zipp and the Big Zipp - are also provided. The Medium Zipp is the fiercest of the three models due to its rigid frame: 6 mm carbon fibre rods for a surface area of 0.52 m² (346 gr/m²). This kite is for the beginner who has had a few basic lessons in stunt kite flying.

Fly it in winds between 3 and 5 Beaufort.

The Big Zipp is the ideal kite for teaching a beginner in extremely light wind conditions (up to 2 Beaufort winds). Despite its lightweight 275 grams and its frame (6 mm carbon fibre), the kite is an absurdly large 1.48 m². Our calculator tells us that the kite weighs 186 grams per square metre, the lightest kite with a frame we know of.

The Big Zipp flies in a calm manner and reacts to commands with ease and precision. Although the 6mm carbon frame is fragile for such a large kite it is extremely flexible and light, which prevents too much breakage, but do not fly the Big Zipp in strong winds.

SPEEDWING SUPER

The Speedwing is meant for traction. It is large and powerful although it does not seem that way compared to many other swept wing delta stunters (1.25 m leading edge, 1.75 m wingspan). It has a substantial camber in the nose and there is a cord on its trailing edge. The Speedwing Super is easier to launch than the original flat Speedwing. Moreover, it flies steadily through the entire wind window and is completely silent. We have modified the bridle so that the kite is easier to adjust and does not turn in a nervous way.

This kite is one of the easiest kites to build, even with the camber construction. As a two- or three-stack, the Speedwing Super is, after the Sputnik 4, the best kite for buggy-riding.

It weighs 300 grams and has a surface area of 0.78 m². The Speedwing Super flies better in 3 - 7 Beaufort winds.

Since certain aspects of the Speedwing are patented the kite may only be built for your private use.

LA HEMBRA

Or 'The Female Beast', performs all the aerobatic manoeuvres described in the chapter on Aerobatics: flips, turtles, axels etc. La Hembra can fly as straight as a die, neither under-steers nor over-steers, and can easily be relaunched from any position.

There are four sail-battens in the sail, giving the kite an attractive round shape, free of any wrinkles.

The performance of the kite changes when whiskers are attached (to tension the trailing edge) or when they are removed. With whiskers, La Hembra becomes an extemely sensitive, aerobatic kite, capable of performing the latest stunts. Without whiskers, La Hembra does not perform as many tricks, but remains a fast and reliable kite in precision flying.

Once launched, you may never want to stop flying this kite again!

We have made La Hembra almost noiseless by using gauze in the wing tips and by threading a cord through the trailing edge. It weighs 300 grams, has a surface area of 0.75 m² and can be flown in winds between 1 - 5 Beaufort.

Caution: this kite is quite complicated to construct.

EL MACHO

'The Muscle Man' has but one objective: to pull, haul or drag you along the beach as hard as possible. For this reason, El Macho has a wing span of more than three metres. It has a surface area of 2 m² and its frame consists of 9 and 10 mm carbon fibre rods.

We have used every possible technique to create this kite: cambers, sail-battens, gauze, cord for the trailing edge, rods that have been bent for the leading edges as well as a 'turbo-bridle'. Despite its size, El Macho is surprisingly easy to steer: it can make perfect ninety degree turns, extreme radical loops and it has superb landing and launching control.

This kite is also a good power source for buggy-riding. You can control the El Macho up to 3-4 Beaufort winds; above that the kite will become your master instead.

KRYPTON-S

This sparless model has been designed for the aspiring Sputnik builder who, nevertheless, still has doubts about his/her sewing skills. The Krypton-S is a power source without frills, a high tech model gone back to basics. Rectangular-shaped, it does not have any gauze in the leading edge air-intake openings.

The profile's centre has an 'S' shape so that the rear half of the wing does not need bridle lines for support.

If you use Icarex P 31 fabric, the kite will weigh 300 grams. It has a surface area of 1.7 m².

The Krypton-S can be flown in winds between 3 and 8 Beaufort.

SPUTNIK 4

For the past two years, we have worked tirelessly on this kite. We based our research on the ideal source of power for 'power-kiting' on Sputniks 1 and 2. Although the Peel (designed by Peter Lynn) is still the best power-kite available on the market, if you want to build your own, the Sputnik 4 is the one you should take.

Sputnik 4 is the only sparless stunt kite we know of with a completely symmetrical profile - the construction of the kite has certainly been simpli-

fied. Unlike the Peel's cross-bridle, the Sputnik 4 has a bow-bridle to decrease weight and drag.

We present three Sputnik designs with tapering wings: 2.2 m², 5 m² and 10 m² variations of the Sputnik 4. We also give measurements for a simple rectangular Sputnik 3 of only 0.8 m², the smallest size which is still comfortable to build and to fly.

PIRAÑA

The world-famous fish etchings of M.C. Escher first inspired us to design and build this floating sculpture. As a *stunt kite* the Piraña is not a superb example. It sways to the left and right, sweeping the sky with its tail as it contemplates the world below with silly bulging eyes. This sort of kite is not built for quality flight performance but for fun. What makes the Piraña so interesting is its shape, not its function.

If you decide to build this kite, not only will it be a test of your construction skills, but also a test of both your perseverance and financial capacity. The stitching is complicated at times, the kite takes weeks not days to produce and you need metres and metres of fabric. One consolation is that the Piraña in this book is small compared to the prototype which is six meters long, five meters high and nine meters wide. We used 120 meters of fabric and it took us three weeks of hard labour to complete!

QUADRIPHANT

This quad-line kite turned out to be an elephant, but it could just as well have been a zebra, a frog or a *Passer Domesticus*. The funny thing about designing quad-line stunt kites is that you can take any direction you want. We felt like making an elephant, so that is what came about. Not only are quad-line kites fun to design, they are also fun to fly or to watch. During the 1993 opening of the International Scheveningen Kite Festival (in the Netherlands) five flyers performed the story of 'Babar the Elephant' with Quadriphants to the accompaniment of live music.

The Quadriphant is easy to manoeuvre and flies in winds as low as 2 Beaufort.

A GUARANTEED HIT?

Even if kites are made according to specific measurements, no two kites are ever identical, nor will they ever fly in the same way. This applies to commercial kites as well: if you were to pick out two kites from a production line at random - say two *Scorpions* from Flexifoil or two *North Shore Radicals* from Top-of-the-Line - these will be seldom, if ever, identical. Yet all commercial kites must be 'guaranteed' to fly, though not all of them are tested beforehand.

Most amateur kite builders swell with pride when their kite flies perfectly on its maiden flight. This is because such luck is considered an exception to the rule. The chance of a successful maiden flight depends to a certain extent on the builder, but the design quality is even more important.

DESIGN QUALITY

By design quality we do not mean an appreciation of the kite's flight-characteristics: for example, a Spin-off flies better than a Flexifoil. What we mean is 'how easily does a Spin-off fly well'? In other words, how many mistakes and inaccuracies is the builder permitted to make without changing the kite's characteristics? Let us compare a Speedwing from *Stunt Kites - To Make and Fly* to a Speedwing from a store. The former flies faster, pulls harder, makes sharper turns. This does not mean it is a better kite; all you have to do is shift the bridle point 2 mm away from the optimal point, make the spreader 1 cm longer or change the direction of the grain of the material and you have a worthless kite. The fact that a kite's characteristics can deteriorate so easily by changes barely noticeable makes this Speedwing design, in fact, inferior to the kite from a store.

QUALITY
OF CONSTRUCTION PLANS

But the case of the fast but sensitive Speedwing can be compensated for by having good construction plans. As long as the builder verifies all the details in the design, he can hardly go wrong. Detailed modifications are provided, so your chances for success in the long run are greater.

TOLERANCE

'Tolerance' is the magic word in the world of mechanics. No two TOTL Hawaiian kites are the same, but they all fall within a certain standard. The maximum and minimum measurements of all parts of a kite are such that no matter how much each part of the kite is varied within that range the kite will still fly. These variations may include the width of the seams, sail measurements, rod lengths, etc. The tighter the tolerance a factory demands, the less variation in

performance the kites produced will display.

Yet tolerance is rarely mentioned in the construction plans for kites. Apart from the template's measurements, the final measurements of a sewn sail should also be given. Of course, you only have to give spinnaker a light tug and your fabric is 1 cm longer. This is often too much for modern stunt kite designs.

The term 'tolerance' in its second meaning also applies here. How far does a design tolerate variations in its measurements? A Spin-off almost always flies, even if you sew it back to front and upside down, so to speak.

The Sputnik in *Stunt Kites - To Make and Fly* is an example of low-tolerance design. Unfortunately, as the designers of the kite, we only discovered later that when such kite models are produced in larger numbers, a certain percentage of them often do not fly as they should. There are many variables to consider: permeability and stretch of fabric, width of seams, consistency in fabric transport when sewing ribs, bridle length, etc.

The new Sputnik 4 design has a much higher tolerance level. Moreover, the entire construction of the kite has been simplified, reducing the chances for inconsistencies considerably.

For instance, the primary bridle lines (the V-lines) of Sputniks 1 and 2 (*Stunt Kites - To Make and Fly*) can either be short (30 cm) or long (120

cm) - a comfortable wide range of tolerance. But in the construction plans, a 30 cm length is given, just too short for good flight performance. Fortunately, most of the flight problems can be solved simply by doubling the length of all the V-lines. The size of the profiles is also right at the limit. Through our experiments over the past few years, we discovered that the profile width can vary between 15 and 19 per cent of the profile length. In the case of Sputniks 1 and 2 it is 18.2 per cent, again close to the limit. If other inconsistencies were to coincide, however, one could imagine this would be all a bit too much.

To conclude, dear reader, set your sights high when you build a kite; but please be tolerant with us, the designers.

In the list of materials for the construction plans, information regarding the type of material used is included. Not only is the type of fabric (nylon or polyester) mentioned, but also the brand name and weight of the fabric. This information has been provided only to give you some idea of what we used; it is not a condition you must adhere to. However, experience has taught us that by using wrong fabric, problems may occur even with models which have never given any trouble before. In Chapter 3 we discussed the various frame and sail materials.

13 ZIPP

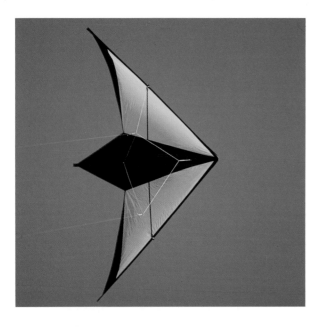

1 The Medium Zipp.

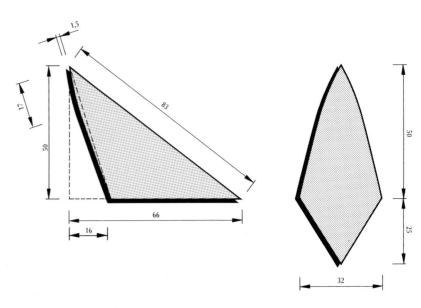

2 Measurements of Zipp.

Wingspan	1.2 m	
Surface area	0.37 m²	
Weight	105 g	
Wind range	2 - 7 Beaufort	
Control lines	←//→ 20 kg	

MATERIALS

0.9 m	spinnaker nylon	
2 pcs	82.5 cm solid carbon fibre, 4 mm Ø	
2 pcs	75 cm solid carbon fibre, 4 mm Ø	
6 pcs	caps, 4 mm internal-Ø	
1 m	Dacron band, 25 mm wide	
2 m	Dacron band, 50 mm wide	
15 cm	reinforced vinyl tubing, 4 mm internal-Ø	
50 cm	kevlar band, 50 mm wide	
2 pcs	clips ←//→ 75 kg	
4 m	bridle line ←//→ 25 kg	

TEMPLATE

Make a template according to the measurements given. The camber billows the most at the point 17 cm from the nose, measuring 1.5 cm. (For details see Chapter 'The Camber'.)

Place the template onto the fabric. The wedge-like central part of the kite is one piece. Pay attention to the grain of the material, exactly perpendicular to the trailing edge of the wings. Add 6 mm to the camber for a flat-fell seam. Add 10 mm to the trailing edge for a folded hem. You now have a sail consisting of three parts: the centre and two wings.

HEMS

Double-fold and sew the trailing edge of the centre and wings to produce a 5 mm wide double hem.

CAMBER

Glue the camber seams with rubber cement and sew together. Now make a flat-fell seam on the reverse side of the kite. Flip the light colour spinnaker onto the darker one.

DACRON BAND

Sew a 25 mm wide Dacron band onto the *front* of the kite (two rows of stitches), about 2 mm from the edge. This strip is meant as reinforcement, not a tunnel for the spine.

WING POCKETS

Fold up the 50 mm Dacron band by hand or by using the folding decive illustrated in *Stunt Kites - To Make and Fly* on page 90. Use the folded Dacron for wing pockets. Push the spinnaker against the Dacron fold and start sewing about

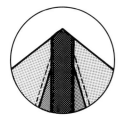

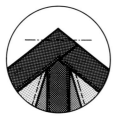

3 *Construction of nose.*

4 *Templates on the cloth.*

5 *Construction of wing tip. The stitching on the inside of the sleeve ends 2 cm before the tip.*

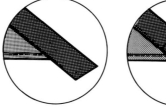

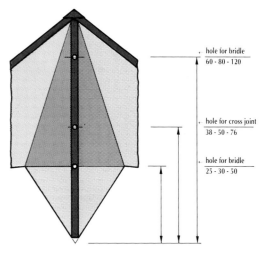

hole for bridle
60 - 80 - 120

hole for cross joint
38 - 50 - 76

hole for bridle
25 - 30 - 50

6 *The centre section, from left to right, measurements for Small, Medium and Big Zipps.*

one centimetre from the nose. Cut off the Dacron when it protrudes at least 5 cm from the wing tips.

NOSE AND TAIL
With extra strong thread and a thick needle, stitch on a piece of folded kevlar. Pay attention to the stitching in the drawing (Cf. Fig. 3). The kevlar should function both as an external pocket for the spine and as an internal stop for the wing spars. The wing spars and spine should lie against each other as rigidly as possible. Cut off any excess kevlar.

Tip: kevlar does not have an attractive colour (dull yellow). For this reason, it is stitched to a piece of Dacron band and this double layer is then stitched onto the nose.

Sew a strong kevlar pocket onto the 25 mm Dacron at the tail side of the kite. Determine

the exact position of the pocket by placing the spine (including end caps!) onto the kite: it should fit nice and taut between nose and tail.

WING TIPS
Push the two wing spars (82.5 cm each) into the pockets and measure the exact length from the pockets (do not forget the end caps). Take out the wing spars. Cut off the Dacron at the proper spot and sew on a piece of folded kevlar or Dacron. Leave a few centimetres of the seam open on the inside (the side of the spine) so that the wing spar can easily be whipped out.

VINYL
Cut three pieces of 4 cm long vinyl tubing. Drill 3 mm holes at the ends of two of the tubes. The third tube is for the cross-fitting:

drill two 3 mm holes perpendicular to each other and 1.5 cm above each other. The spine will be placed through the lower hole, the cross spar through the higher hole.

HOLES
Hot-tack three holes into the centre of the Dacron, either with a hot-tacker or a thick, glowing nail. Shove the T-fitting onto the spine, push the spine into the nose and tail and push the T-fitting through the hole in the middle.

Place the wing spars in the pockets.

Push the spine (the remaining 75 cm length of carbon fibre) through the T-fitting until the T-fitting is exactly in the middle of the spine. With a pencil, mark the precise position where the cross spar touches the wing spars.

Take the frame out again and hot-tack holes on the pencil-mark spots.

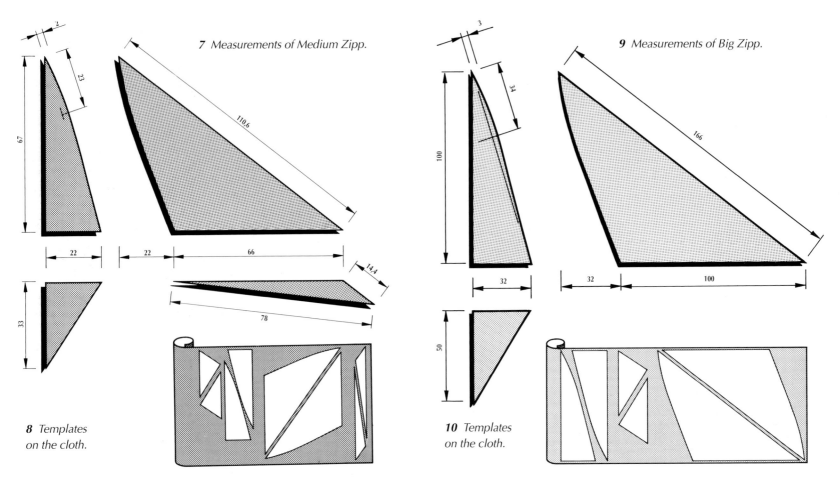

7 Measurements of Medium Zipp.

9 Measurements of Big Zipp.

8 Templates on the cloth.

10 Templates on the cloth.

BRIDLE

The bridle consists of a long main bridle and two short secondary ones. For the secondary bridles measure two pieces of 75 cm lengths. With an overhand knot on both lines make a loop of approximately 8 cm. At the other end make two short loops of approximately 2 cm. The total length of each bridle should be 49 cm. The longer loop will later be placed over the wing spars, the smaller ones being attached to the clips.

For the main bridle use 2.5 m of line. Fold the line over and make an overhand loop of about 9 cm in the middle. At 57 cm away from the middle make a mark where the clips will come. Now make two 3 cm overhand loops at the two loose ends. The total length of the main bridle should be 109 cm.

Push the middle of the main bridle through the hole on the nose end of the kite and the two loose ends through the holes on the tail

end. Attach them to the spine of the kite (at the back) with lark's heads and place the spine in its pocket. Mount the cross spar. The kite is ready.

TIPS

The Medium Zipp and the Big Zipp are made in the same way as the basic Zipp. Measurements for the kite and bridle are self-explanatory. We made the hem of the Big Zipp wider: 10 mm instead of 5 mm. This way it is easier to place a

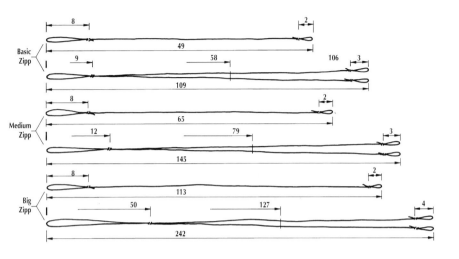

Basic Zipp
8 ... 49 ... 2
9 ... 58 ... 106 ... 3
109

Medium Zipp
8 ... 65 ... 2
12 ... 79 ... 3
145

Big Zipp
8 ... 113 ... 2
50 ... 127 ... 4
242

12 Bridle lines of all Zipps.

11 The nose: the spine is tucked into an open pocket.

more economically from the fabric. The spinnaker nylon is perpendicular to the trailing edge.

The camber in the centre section is used to draw the camber of the wings. See chapter 'The Camber'.

line through the trailing edge of the wings and the centre section in order to get rid of any last rustling sounds the kite may make. For those of you attentive readers: indeed, to make the Big Zipp we simply multiplied the measurements of the basic Zipp by two.

The Medium Zipp came about when we decided to make a Zipp with 100 and 125 cm rods.

Our centre section of the Medium and Big Zipp consists of four pieces so that this section can be cut

---

MEDIUM ZIPP

Wingspan	1.8 m
Surface area	0.52 m²
Weight	180 g
Wind range	3 - 5 Beaufort
Control lines	←//→ 30 - 35 kg

MATERIALS

1.2 m	spinnaker nylon
2 pcs	1 m carbon fibre rods, 6 mm Ø
2 pcs	1.25 m carbon fibre rods, 6 mm Ø
6 pcs	end caps, 5 mm internal-Ø
1.5 m	Dacron band, 25 mm wide
3 m	Dacron band, 50 mm wide
20 cm	reinforced vinyl tube, 6 mm internal-Ø
50 cm	kevlar band, 50 mm wide
2 pcs	clips ←//→ 75 kg
5 m	bridle line ←//→ 50 kg

BIG ZIPP

Wingspan	2.4 m
Surface area	1.48 m²
Weight	275 g
Wind range	1 - 3 Beaufort
Control lines	←//→ 40 - 60 kg

MATERIALS

2 m	spinnaker nylon
2 pcs	1.5 m carbon fibre rods, 6 mm Ø
2 pcs	1.65 m carbon fibre rods, 6 mm Ø
6 pcs	end caps, 5 mm internal-Ø
2 m	Dacron band, 25 mm wide
4 m	Dacron band, 50 mm wide
20 cm	reinforced vinyl tubing, 6 mm internal-Ø
50 cm	kevlar band, 50 mm wide
2 pcs	clips ←//→ 75 kg
8 m	bridle line ←//→ 65 kg

14 SPEEDWING SUPER

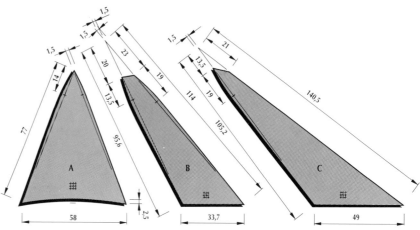

1 *Measurements of the three templates.*

2 *Details construction leading edge sleeve.*

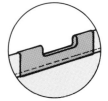

Wingspan	1.8 m
Surface area	0.78 m²
Weight	300 g
Wind range	3 - 7 Beaufort
Control lines	←//→ 90 - 135 kg

MATERIALS

1.5 m	spinnaker nylon (Carrington)
2 pcs	1.25 m carbon fibre tubing 9 mm Ø, thick-walled
1 pc	1.25 m carbon fibre tubing 10 mm Ø
1 pc	1 m glassfibre tubing 12 mm Ø
15 cm	reinforced vinyl tubing, 9 mm internal-Ø
20 cm	reinforced vinyl tubing, 10 mm internal-Ø
3 m	Dacron band, 60 mm width
50 cm	Dacron band, 20 mm width
8 m	bridle line, ←//→ 135 kg
2 pcs	clips, ←//→ 135 kg
1 pc	aluminum ring
2 pcs	end caps, 9 mm internal-Ø

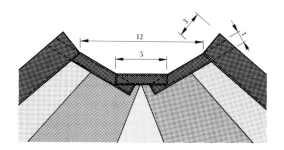

3 *Construction of the nose. Pieces of Dacron are first attached to the sides, then to the centre.*

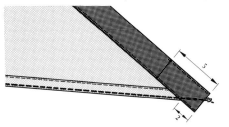

4 *The Super with measurements of holes for the spreader.*

5 *Leading edge sleeve with details of tips and tensioning cord.*

6 *Bridle lines.*

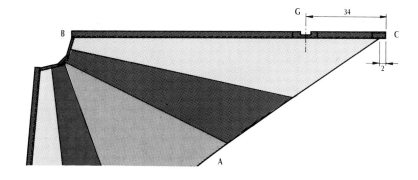

7 *Cross-strut fitting*

TEMPLATE

Make three templates according to the measurements given in Figure 1 and place them on the spinnaker fabric. Cut out one piece of fabric using template A (for the centre) and two pieces of fabric using templates B and C. Mind the grain of the material. Note that the 1 cm camber seam and the 1.5 cm hem of the trailing edge are included in the measurements.

CAMBER

If necessary, glue the camber seams with rubber cement and then stitch together 1 cm from the edge. Make a flat-stitched seam on the reverse side of the material. Fold the lighter coloured fabric onto the darker one.

Always start sewing from the trailing edge towards the nose so that the kite has an even trailing edge. Should the nose show unevenness you can always eliminate this later with a soldering iron.

TRAILING EDGE

Fold the trailing edge twice and stitch to give a 10 mm wide double hem.

NOSE

Because the nose of the Speedwing Super is round, its construction differs from a standard Speedwing. Double-fold a piece of 2 cm-wide Dacron. Divide the Dacron into three pieces: two 15 cm strips and one 5 cm strip. Stitch the longer strips onto the sides of the nose twice and the shorter strip onto the middle, overlapping the strips on the sides. Cut off the protruding ends diagonally along the sides.

LEADING EDGE SLEEVES

Fold over the 60 mm Dacron (by hand or with a folding device). Double up the first two centimetres of the Dacron sleeve and start sewing from the nose, working your way down towards the trailing edge. Make sure both sleeves start at the same distance from the nose and place the nylon all the way in to the fold of the Dacron sleeve. The width of the nose between the two sleeves should be 12 cm. Cut off the sleeve at Point C in a straight line. At Point C sew on a double layer of Dacron band. Cut two 10 cm pieces from the

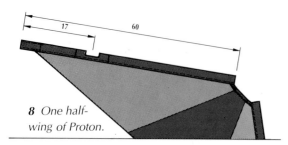

8 One half-wing of Proton.

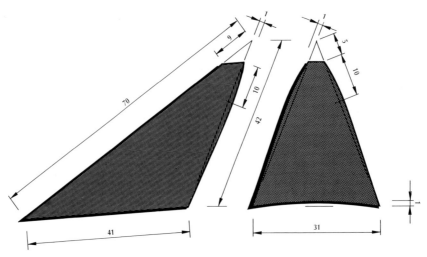

9 The Proton measurements include a 5 mm seam along the profile and 2 x 5 mm hem at the trailing edge.

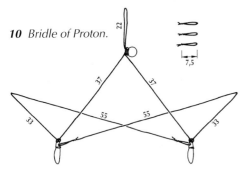

10 Bridle of Proton.

leftover Dacron band and sew them onto the leading edges, starting 29 cm from Point C. With a template, cut out a hole at Point G, 34 cm from Point C.

NOSE PIECE

Cut a 10 cm piece of vinyl tube with a 9 mm internal diameter. This is for the nose piece. Drill or punch a hole in the middle of the tube. Cut off 4 rings, each 1 cm wide, from the left-over vinyl tubing.

PROTON	
Wingspan	87 cm
Surface area	0.19 m²
Weight	64 g
Wind range	2 - 6 Beaufort
Control lines	←//→ 20 kg

BRIDLE

Cut three 30 cm long lines and using an over-hand knot make three loops of equal length from these. Make a 370 cm line and two 105 cm lines; the measurements include 10 cm loops at each end.

CROSS-STRUT FITTINGS

The cross-strut fittings consist of two 10 cm pieces of reinforced vinyl tubing. Drill or punch two 8 mm holes as shown in Figure 7.

ASSEMBLY

1 Push one of the three loops through the hole of the nose piece and make a lark's head.
2 Slide the cross-strut fitting with vinyl rings on each side onto each leading edge spar. Place end caps at the ends of each spar. Push one of the spars through the hole at G to the top of the kite at B; then squeeze it through the re-maining 30 cm of leading edge hem. Repeat the procedure with the other spar. Push both spars into the nose piece.
3 With a lark's head attach the remaining two loops onto both cross-strut fittings.
4 With a lark's head attach the centre of the long bridle line to the loop on the nose piece.
5 With a lark's head attach the ends of the long bridle line to the loops around the cross-strut fittings.
6 With a lark's head attach the bridle clips to the long line, about 70 cm from Point G.
7 With a lark's head attach the loops of the shorter (diagonal) lines at Z to the loops around the cross-strut fittings and, at the other ends, to the clips.
8 Attach an aluminum ring with a lark's head on the long line, 40 cm from the top at B.
9 Push the cross spars into the fittings. Make sure that the distance between the cross spar and Point A is approximately 38 cm. If the distance is shorter the kite's sail is tensioned too much; lower the fittings from the nose downwards. If the distance is longer, then the sail is too slack; push the fittings towards the kite's nose. When you have reached the optimum billowing of the sail, glue the vinyl rings so that the fittings cannot shift. The kite is ready.

11 The measurements of the Speedwing 3 x 1 include a 7 mm seam for the profile and 2 x 7 mm for the trailing edge.

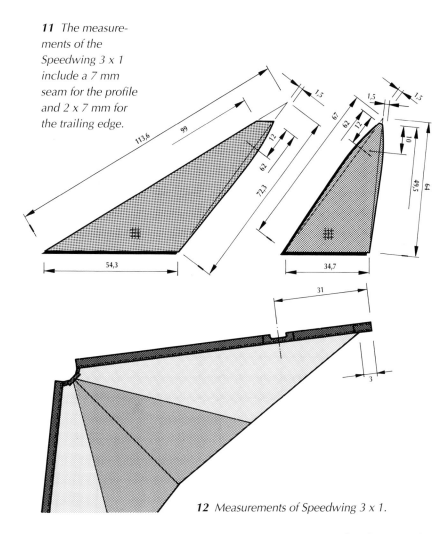

12 Measurements of Speedwing 3 x 1.

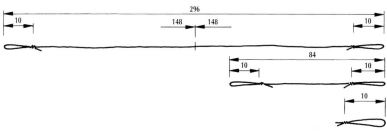

13 Bridle of the 3 x 1; aluminum ring 32 cm from the nose, bridle clips 60 cm from the cross-strut fittings.

the distance between the control lines is shorter, making the Super easier to manoeuvre.

Thirdly, the bridle is not attached directly to the frame but to loose loops attached to the frame with lark's heads. This makes it much easier to remove the bridle lines if necessary (when stacking kites for instance).

In the list of materials is a 1 m glass-fibre tube. If the cross spar bends too much (e.g. in winds stronger than 4 Beaufort), this tube can be placed over the cross spar to give additional strength.

The list of materials also mentions 9 mm-diameter carbon fibre tubing with thick walls. We tried using 9 mm and 10 mm tubing in some of the Speedwing Super prototypes, but found that in strong winds both tubes snapped immediately at the cross-strut fittings: 9 mm-diameter tubing with thick walls solved the problem.

Finally, a note about noise. Despite the deep billow of the sail, the kite may not be completely soundless. To silence it further, string a thin line through the hem of the trailing edge of the kite. (See chapter 'The Camber').

As a bonus we have listed the measurements for a miniature version of the Speedwing Super, the Proton. To do this we divided all the measurements of the Speedwing Super into two. For the frame three pieces of 62.5 cm long, 4 mm solid carbon fibre are used, both for the leading edges as well as the spine.

The kite's sail consists of three panels instead of five, and has two camber seams.

The Speedwing 3 x 1 is based on a frame of three 1 m carbon tubing; 6 or 7 mm Ø for the wingspars and 8 mm Ø for the spreader. The sail consists of four panels and has three camber seams.

TIPS

There are three characteristics that distinguish the Speedwing Super from the Speedwing in our first book.

First, the sail billows more so that the kite pulls harder and more consistently and is easier to launch.

Secondly, the main bridle is comparatively longer and the diagonal bridles shorter. Thus

SPEEDWING 3 X 1	
Wingspan	1,5 m
Surface area	0.5 m²
Weight	175 g
Wind range	2 - 7 Beaufort
Control lines	←//→ 40 - 90 kg

15 LA HEMBRA

Wingspan	2.2 m
Surface area	0.75 m²
Weight	300 g
Wind range	1 - 5 Beaufort
Control lines	←//→ 50 - 75 kg

MATERIALS

3 pcs	carbon fibre tubing 150 cm, 6 mm Ø	
1 pc	carbon fibre tubing 165 cm, 6 mm Ø	
2 pcs	solid carbon fibre rods 150 cm, 1.5 mm Ø	
2 pcs	solid carbon fibre rods 150 cm, 2 mm Ø	
0.5 m	spinnaker, colour 1 Icarex P-31	
0.5 m	spinnaker, colour 2 Icarex P-31	
0.3 m	spinnaker, colours 3 and 4 combined Icarex P-31	
0.1 m	spinnaker, colours 5 and 5 combined Icarex P-31	
0.5 m	gauze, 10 cm wide	
4 m	Dacron band, 5 cm wide	
2.5 m	Dacron band, 3 cm wide	
1 m	Dacron band, 2 cm wide	
10 m	Dacron band, 1.25 cm wide	
0.5 m	Kevlar band, 5 or 6 cm wide	
1 m	bungee cord and a piece of elastic band	
4 pcs	vinyl cross spar connectors 6 mm	
1 pc	central cross-fitting 3 x 6 mm	
2 pcs	vinyl whisker connectors or strong vinyl tubing, 3 mm Ø	
3 pcs	end caps with slits 6 mm	
3 pcs	vinyl end caps 6 mm	
8 pcs	vinyl end caps 2 mm	
2 pcs	bridle clips, ←//→ 75 kg	
12 m	bridle line, ←//→ 75 kg	
0.1 m	vinyl tube, 4 mm Ø	

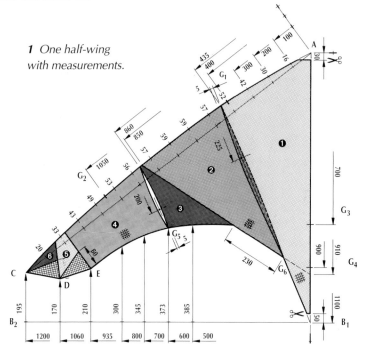

1 One half-wing with measurements.

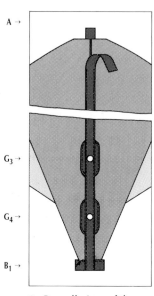

2 Overall view of the central section.

Do not worry if your local kite store does not have the exact items listed above; the sail-battens and whiskers can also be made from glass-fibre rods one size thicker. Dacron band of other widths is fine too. Do not hesitate to change details. Regarding the carbon fibre rods for the frame, preferably choose a High Modulus carbon fibre type (e.g. RCF-Ultra or Skyshark), except for the cross spar (2 x 75 cm). It is better to make this part from a standard rod.

TEMPLATE

One half of La Hembra wing consists of eight panels. In order to retain all the exact measurements of these sections, it is important to first draw one wing-half completely onto a sheet of cardboard. First draw the base line from B1 to B2 and the middle line from A to B1 onto the cardboard.

Then find Point C and draw a straight line from A to C. From this line dots are placed at 10 cm intervals so that the final wing contour from Point A to C can be drawn smoothly with the help of a fibreglass rod. Only the transition from Panel 1 to Panel 2 should not be smooth (but you will see that after sewing the camber seam between Panels 1 and 2, the transition will be smooth). Now all the remaining measurements can be made according to the drawing. Note that the camber between 1 and 2 is, like most cambers, a convex, i.e. there is an 'extra' 5 mm of fabric at the highest point. The camber between 3 and 4, on the other hand, is 'hollow'. Here the fabric is actually concave: 5 mm less at the deepest point. This is to prevent wrinkles from forming when the wings are tensioned by whiskers. The wedge-like pieces at A and B1 can be cut away.

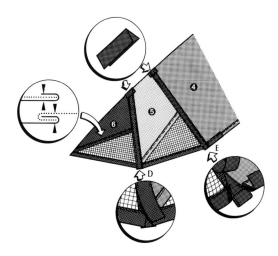

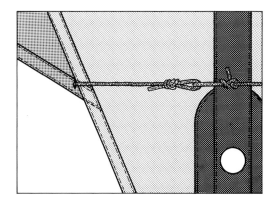

3 Wing tip.

CUTTING

To make this kite it is advisable to use polyester fabric, Icarex P31. It is not necessary to hot-cut this type of material. However, when Dacron band is cut to size it should be hot-cut. The grain of the material should, as usual, be perpendicular to the trailing edge. Note that both panels have a camber allowance. If you cut the templates out of one sheet of card board (as we have advised), one of the two panels will have a hollow camber. Use the other panel (with the billowing camber) in order to draw the correct curvature onto the spinnaker. (See Chapter 'The Camber'.)

Panels 3 and 4 each have a 5 to 7 mm allowance at their connecting seams and 15 mm at the trailing edges. Panels 5 and 6 are partly made from gauze. To connect the two materials with a double flat stitched seam you need an allowance of 15 mm for the gauze and 7 mm for spinnaker.

4 Reverse side of kite with knot in the tensioning cord.

SEWING ORDER

Keep the following directions near your sewing machine as the correct sewing order is crucial to the kite's construction. The following refers to one wing only, the other half is self-evident. However, remember to keep the symmetry in mind.

1 Connect 3 and 4 with a 'hollow' camber seam. Place the pieces flat on top of each other and sew together, 5 mm from the edge (seam allowance). Open out the fabric, fold the protruding edge flat (onto the darker colour) and sew on. Then a 7 mm trailing edge is folded over twice and sewn. Leave some space for the threading of the tension cord later.

2 Tips 5 and 6 are made by joining the gauze and spinnaker with a double flat stitched seam and by hemming the bottom edge with Dacron (the 2 cm wide Dacron band folded over). The joint between 5 and 6 is

used later as a sleeve for a sail-batten. Start with a strip of 1 cm Dacron, use a strip of double-sided tape to glue on the panels 5 and 6, then a second piece of Dacron is placed over this. The sleeve is sewn close to the edges to leave room for the sail-batten. To prevent fraying, fold the Dacron in at the lower end. Close the tunnel at the top by stitching a piece of Kevlar band over it.

3 The finished wing tip can now be sewn onto Panel 4 in the same way, but before you do this sew a small strip (4 cm) of folded 2 cm Dacron onto Point E of Panel 4 (a tension cord will later be threaded through). The second sail-batten tunnel is ready.

4 Now return to the centre seam. Glue Panels 1 of both left and right wings flush to each other on a strip of 3 cm wide Dacron. Next place a strip of 12 x 5 cm Dacron band with rounded ends at G3 and at G4, a strip of folded 5 cm Dacron band onto B1 and sew these reinforcements all the way round. Finally, place the second strip of 3 cm Dacron over the entire length and sew on. This is the tunnel for the spine.

5 The joint between 1 and 2 is made the same way. However, use a strip of 1 cm wide Dacron band instead. This sail-batten tunnel should extend to and include 1 cm of the Dacron reinforcement at B1. Sew a piece of elastic band onto this tip so that the sail-batten can maintain the tension on the sail. Close the tunnel at the wing edge with Kevlar band.

6 Panels 2 and 3 are joined in the same way. At G6 leave a small opening at the tunnel for the sail-batten and tension cord.

7 The wing spar tunnel is sewn with 5 cm Dacron band in the traditional manner; the fabric is pushed against and into the fold of the folded Dacron band. The nose also gets the usual treatment with Dacron and a double layer of Kevlar.

8 You need to add a piece of Dacron reinforcement at G5 - hot-cut a circle of 25 mm Ø Dacron, fold it over the hem and sew around, leaving the bottom hem open.

ASSEMBLY

With the help of a small template, first hot-cut large holes at G1, G2, G3 and G4. B1, C and G5 get small holes, but large enough for the 3 mm bungee cords and whiskers. Now mount the frame with the necessary cross connectors and protection caps. The leading edges are made from 150 cm tubing, the spreaders from two halves of a 150 cm tube and the spine - together with the top spreader - from a 165 cm tube. To prevent sliding, glue retainers to the cross-fitting at G3 and the connectors at G1.

Now comes the tricky part: thread the tension line through the trailing edge of the kite with a darning needle. For each wing begin at Point C, go through the seam to D, through the top of the 2 mm end cap, back through the seam to E, through the end cap once again, then back into the seam for the long stretch via part of the sail-batten tunnel to G6. At that point leave the tunnel from the back. At C tie a loop for the split nock and let the other end at G6 hang free for the time being.

Now all the sail-battens are made to size and placed accordingly: a 2 mm batten between B1 and G1 - tensioned with elastic band - and a 1.5 mm batten in the tunnel from G6 to the wing spar, tightly held in place with a piece of vinyl tubing at G4. From the remaining pieces of carbon rods, make sail-battens for D and E which can be tightened with the help of end caps and tension cord. After making the whiskers to size using the remaining 2 mm carbon fibre at G5, the entire kite is assembled and the tension cords having this far been hanging loosely can be tied together under tension. A nice and tight keel-shaped kink should appear at the centre section of the kite.

5 *Wing tip.*

6 *The keel is created by tightening the tensioning cord; four sail-battens make La Hembra billow nicely.*

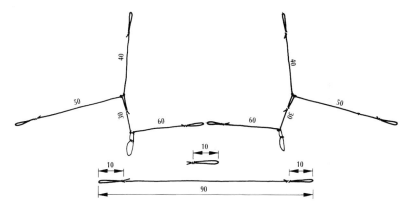

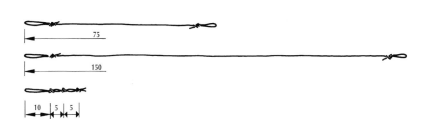

7 *The measurements for a standard bridle configuration.*

8 *Optional: the 'turbo' bridle.*

BRIDLE

First tie six loops with three overhand knots, as per the measurements given. A loop is attached to G1 and G2 respectively with a lark's head and two are attached to the cross-fitting at G3. Knot the short and long bridle lines and attach these with lark's heads to the central knots of each loop. A bridle clip is placed halfway down the long lines between G3 and G1, the short line connecting this bridle clip to G2.

Finally, an extra connecting line is used halfway down the upper bridle lines to slightly 'pinch' them together (see Chapter 'The Bridle').

ADJUSTMENTS

Adjusting the bridle hardly needs explaining - because of the deep curvature in the sail, La Hembra allows plenty of room for adjustment.

The knots on the attachment loops can be used to experiment with various positions for the bridle clips: placing them further away from each other, or nearer to the centre. La Hembra easily adapts to such modifications by subtly altering its flying characteristics. We recommend you experiment with various possibilities before adjusting the bridle to suit your preferences.

TIPS

La Hembra can endure strong winds even when made from fragile High-Modulus carbon fibre tubing, but you certainly need strong nerves to fly the kite under such conditions. The harder the wind blows, the faster the kite will turn - add a strong pull to

that and you have an exciting kite but potentially dangerous weapon. La Hembra should, therefore, be flown in extremely light winds (we later modified La Hembra, creating a true power kite : El Macho. See chapter 'El Macho').

An even larger version of La Hembra with a three piece Skyshark leading edge spar can be used in stacks as a traction-kite for buggy-riding in extremely light winds.

It is not necessary to fly La Hembra with whiskers; the sail-battens keep the sail sufficiently tensioned so that the kite is constantly under control. In fact, without whiskers La Hembra flies even better. The kite is also extemely suitable for team flying. However, when performing most of the tricks - such as those mentioned in the chapter 'Aerobatics' - whiskers are indispensable.

16 EL MACHO

Wingspan	3.05 m
Surface area	2 m²
Weight	740 g
Wind range	2 - 7 Beaufort
Control lines	←//→ 90 - 150 kg

MATERIALS

2 pcs	200 cm carbon fibre, 9 mm Ø thick-walled
1 pc	150 cm carbon fibre, 9 mm Ø
2 pcs	100 cm carbon fibre, 10 mm Ø
1 pc	82.5 cm carbon fibre, 8 mm Ø
4 pcs	150 cm solid carbon fibre, 2 mm Ø
1.5 m	spinnaker, colour 1 Icarex PL-62
0.8 m	spinnaker, colour 2 Icarex PL-62
0.8 m	spinnaker, colours 3 and 4 Carrington 42 gr
0.2 m	spinnaker, colours 5 and 6 Carrington 42 gr
0.5 m	gauze, 10 cm wide
6 m	Dacron band, 6 cm wide
3.5 m	Dacron band, 4 cm wide
1 m	Dacron band, 2 cm wide
10 m	Dacron band, 1.5 cm wide
0.5 m	Kevlar band, 5 or 6 cm wide
1.5 m	elastic band, 3 mm wide
0.2 m	reinforced vinyl tubing, 8, 9 and 10 mm internal-Ø
1 pc	connector, 10 mm internal-Ø
3 pcs	arrow nocks with slits 9 mm Ø
1 pc	end cap with slit 6 mm Ø
3 pcs	end caps, 9 mm Ø
8 pcs	end caps, 2 mm Ø
2 pcs	bridle clips, ←//→ 135 kg
8 m	bridle line, ←//→ 135 kg
5 m	line for hem on trailing edge, ←//→ 50 kg double-sided tape

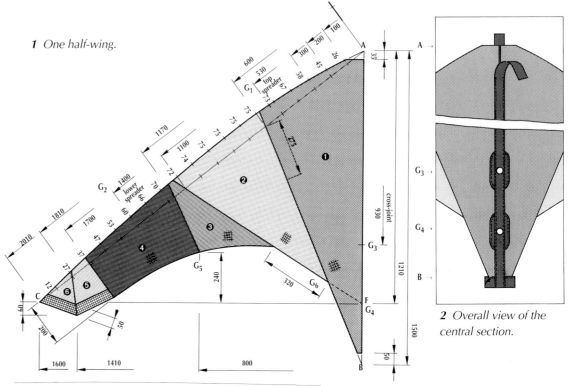

1 One half-wing.

2 Overall view of the central section.

Do not worry if your local kite store does not have the exact items listed above; the sail-battens and whiskers can also be made from glass-fibre rods one size thicker. Dacron band of other widths is fine too. Do not hesitate to change details. Use the 2 m, thick-walled carbon fibre rods for the leading edges; if you want to divide them into two parts, you will need two additional connectors. If your local kite store does not stock 2 m rods, purchase two 1.5 m rods and one 1 m rod. Use the two 10 mm Ø carbon fibre rods for the cross spars, the rest of the 9 mm Ø standard rod for the spine and the 8 mm Ø rod for the top spreader.

The rods for the lower spreaders are filled with a piece of 8 mm Ø carbon fibre rod at the cross-joint.

TEMPLATE

One half of the wing of El Macho consists of eight panels. In order to retain the exact measurements of these sections, it is important to first draw one wing-half onto a piece of cardboard. Unlike La Hembra, we will be using a different method to construct the template for this kite, otherwise the piece of cardboard will be too big for the work-ing-table.

First draw a line from C to F (160 cm) and from A to F (121 cm); use the edge of the cardboard for this. Then draw a line from A to C (201 cm). You now have the basic triangle. Dots are placed at 10 cm intervals from the line A to C so that the final wing contour from points A to C can be drawn smoothly with the aid of a fibreglass rod. Only the

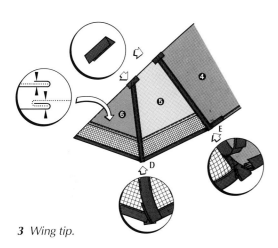

3 Wing tip.

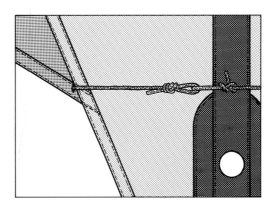

4 Reverse side of kite with knot in the tightening cord.

transition from Panel 1 to Panel 2 is not smooth (but you will see that after sewing the camber seam between Panels 1 and 2, the transition will be smooth). Now all the remaining measurements can be made as in Figure 1. Note that the camber between 1 and 2 is convex like most cambers: i.e. there is an 'extra' 7 mm of fabric at the highest point. El Macho does not have a camber between 3 and 4 because the kite is flown without whiskers. The wedge-like pieces at A and B can be cut away.

The triangles from B to F to C are made from leftover cardboard and taped onto the basic triangle.

CUTTING

To make this kite, we used Icarex PL 62, a polyester fabric coated on one side with a layer of Mylar, giving it a shiny look. Because the other side of the fabric is dull, it cannot be used so you need more fabric to make the kite. In the case of regular spinnaker, both sides of the fabric can be used, making it a more efficient material.

The grain of the material should be, as usual, as perpendicular to the trailing edge as possible.

Panels 1 and 2 are sewn into the Dacron band and do not need any sewing allowance. But note that both panels have a camber allowance. If you cut both templates out of a single piece of cardboard (as we have recommended), one of the two panels will have a hollow camber. Use the other panel (with the billowing camber) to draw the correct curvature onto the fabric. (See chapter 'The Camber'.)

Panels 3 and 4 each have a 7 mm allowance at their connecting seams and 15 mm at their trailing edges. Parts of panels 6 and 7 are made of gauze. To connect the two materials with a double flat stitched seam, you need an allowance of 15 mm of gauze and 7 mm of spinnaker nylon.

Note: We prefer to use the softer Carrington to create a more natural shape on the wing tips.

SEWING ORDER

Keep the following directions near your sewing machine - the correct sewing order is crucial for the kite's construction. We strongly advise not to unpick seams in Mylar fabric - the perforations will remain visible and the fabric becomes weak. Use double-sided tape for gluing and large stitches for sewing. The following refers only to one wing-half - the other half is self-evident. However, keep the symmetry in mind.

1 Connect 4 and 3 with a felled seam. Place the sections on top of each other and sew together, leaving a 7 mm seam allowance at the edge. Open out the material, push the protruding edge down (towards the darker colour) and sew it on. Now a 7 mm trailing edge hem is double-folded and sewn. Keep some space for the tension cord to be threaded through the seam later.

2 Tips 5 and 6 are both made by joining the gauze and spinnaker with a double flat stitched seam and by hemming the bottom edge with Dacron - the 2 cm wide Dacron band folded over. The joint between 5 and 6 will eventually function as a sleeve for the sail-batten. First attach a strip of double-sided tape onto a strip of 1.5 cm Dacron, then glue both pieces so that they join at the centre of the Dacron. A second strip of Dacron is placed over this. The sleeve is sewn close to the edges. To prevent fraying, fold the Dacron in at the lower end. Close the tunnel at the top by stitching a piece of Kevlar band over it.

3 The entire tip piece can now be sewn onto Panel 4 in the same manner, but first sew a small strip (4 cm) of folded 2 cm Dacron onto Point E of Panel 4 (a tension cord will eventually be threaded here). The second sail-batten tunnel is ready.

4 Now we return to the centre seam. Glue Panel 1 of both left and right wings flush to each other on a strip of 4 cm wide Dacron. Next

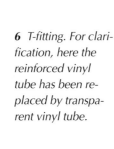

5 Two sail-battens come together in a plastic end-cap.

6 T-fitting. For clarification, here the reinforced vinyl tube has been replaced by transparent vinyl tube.

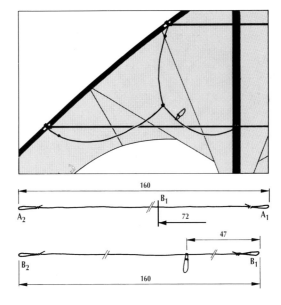

7 Measurements of the 'turbo' bridle.

8 Extenders elongate the lower spreaders.

place a strip of 12 x 6 cm Dacron band with rounded ends at G3 and G4, and a strip of 6 cm Dacron band folded over B. Sew these reinforcement pieces all the way round. Finally, place the second strip of 4 cm Dacron onto the entire length and sew on. This is the tunnel for the spine.

5   The joint between Panels 1 and 2 is made in the same way. However, use a strip of 1.5 cm wide Dacron band instead. This sail-batten tunnel should extend to and include 1 cm of the Dacron reinforcement at B. Close the tunnel at the leading edge with Kevlar band.

6   Panels 3 and 2 are joined in the same way. At G6 keep a small opening at the entrance of the tunnel for the sail-batten and tension cord. For the neatest result, have the strip of Dacron at the reverse side of the kite stick-

ing out. Stop the strip of Dacron at the front of the kite at G6. See Figure 4.

7   The wing spar tunnel is sewn with 6 cm Dacron band in the traditional manner. The fabric is pushed against and into the folded Dacron band. The nose also gets the standard treatment of Dacron and a double layer of Kevlar.

CROSS-JOINT

You will have to make the cross-joint for this kite yourself. Use a piece of reinforced vinyl tubing with a 10 mm internal diameter and a length of approximately 6 cm. First make a 8 mm Ø hole on the inside. The 9 mm spine will come here. Make a 9 mm hole, 2 cm from and perpendicular to the first hole. The connector to join the two cross-struts comes here. With a pair of pliers, make a small dent in the middle

of the connector. This will keep the cross-struts from sliding all the way through.

ASSEMBLY

With the help of a small template, first hot-cut the large holes at G1, G2, G3 and G4. Make sure there is about 1 cm of space between G1 and the piece of Kevlar in the sleeve (see point 5). B and C get smaller holes, large enough for the 3 mm bungee cords. Now mount the frame with the necessary cross-joints and protection caps. To prevent sliding, glue retainers to the cross-fitting at G3 and to the joints at G1.

Now comes the tricky part: thread the tension line through the trailing edge of the kite with a darning needle. For each wing begin at Point C, go through the seam to D, go through the top of the 2 mm end cap, back through the seam to E, through the end cap once again,

9 *The tip.*

10 *Vinyl cross-joint.*

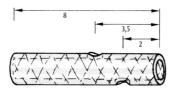

then back into the seam for the long stretch via part of the sail-batten tunnel to G6. At that point leave the tunnel from the back. At C tie a loop for the split nock and, for the time being, let the other end at G6 hang free.

Now all the sail-battens are made to size and placed accordingly: a 2 mm batten between B and G1 - tensioned with elastic band on a 6 mm end cap (see illustration) - and a 2 mm batten in the tunnel from G6 to the wing spar. It is tightly held in place at G4, either with a piece of reinforced vinyl tubing or with two whisker joints. From the remaining pieces of carbon rods, make sail-battens for D and E which can be tightened with the end caps and tension cord. Now the tension cords that have been hanging loosely can be tied together and tensioned. A nice and tight keel-shaped kink appears at the centre section of the kite.

BRIDLE
First tie six loops with three overhand knots, as per the measurements given. A loop is attached to G1 and G2 respectively with a lark's head and two are attached to the cross-fitting at G3.

Knot the four main lines, each 160 cm long. Lines A run from the top spreader (A1) to the lower spreader (A2). Lines B run from the cross-joint (B2) to the marked points on lines A. The clips come on line B (Cf. Figure 7).

ADJUSTMENTS
Thanks to the special bridle of this kite, El Macho is easy to manoeuvre. The turns are so fast you will hardly be able to follow the kite with your eyes. If you want the kite to turn slower, make a standard bridle, in which case the main lines should be 200 cm long, the lines on the side 120 cm.

If you place the clips on the designated markings nothing can go wrong. The kite, however, will tolerate minor adjustments anywhere near the marks.

By mounting longer lower spreaders (105 cm), the kite becomes noticeably faster. In fact, the kite will also tend to over-steer. When attempting a half spin it will spin a full circle instead before responding to your command. With a standard lower spreader of 100 cm El Macho becomes slower but more reliable.

Do not place the upper spreader too tightly between the leading edges or you may push the billowing shape out of the nose. The kite will then be difficult to launch.

TIPS
The 2 m leading edges make El Macho rather difficult to transport. Sew the rods in two, 50 cm

11 *Buggying with El Macho.*

away from the tips. One and a half metres of rod remains in the sleeve, the remaining 50 cm is taken out. The two rods are connected with a connector 10 cm long and a 9 mm internal diameter. By dividing the rods at the points we mentioned (and not, for example, halfway down the rods), the vinyl cross-joints of the upper- and lower spreaders can remain where they are. Moreover, by removing the ends of the leading edges, the short sail-battens by the tips can be folded against the kite.

17 KRYPTON-S

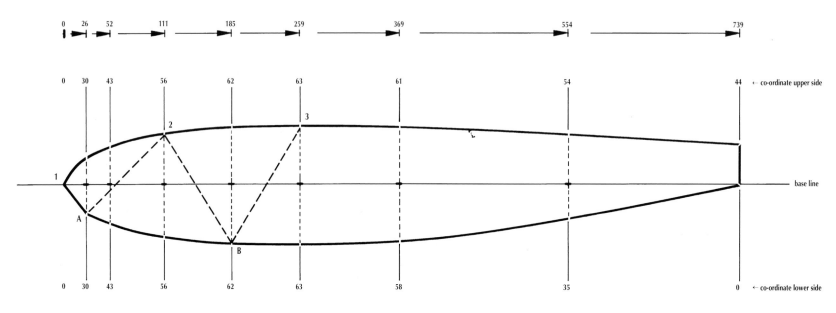

1 *Profile of a Krypton-S, 25 per cent of its true size.*

Wing span	240 cm
Aspect Ratio	3.25
Surface area	1.7 m²
Weight	300 g
Wind range	3 - 8 Beaufort
Control lines	←//→ 75 to 150 kg

MATERIALS

4 m	Carrington spinnaker nylon 150 cm wide
35 m	braided Dacron bridle line ←//→ 50 kg
2.5 m	braided Dacron bridle line ←//→ 200 kg

CUTTING / DRAWING

Top and bottom of the wing are made from a single piece of spinnaker nylon, of 241 cm length and of at least 150 cm width. Start by drawing the 25 vertical lines at 10 cm intervals (plus 0.5 cm for the hem on both sides) on the fabric. Then cut the fabric in the middle so that you get two long strips, one for the top and one for the bottom. The top layer should be at least 76 cm wide, the bottom at least 74 cm wide. If the fabric is wider than 150 cm, make both strips wider. Draw the profile co-ordinates onto the template according to the figure. First draw a base line from 0 to 739 mm, then mark the co-ordinates towards the top and bottom as per the intervals shown. Now connect the points in a smooth line. Clearly mark at Points A, B, 1, 2 and 3 onto the cardboard. Note: the measurements of this template include seam allowances!

With the help of the template cut out the 25 ribs. With a soft pencil transfer the five marks onto each rib.

SEWING

First hem in the short straight sides at the noses of the ribs. Fold over 5 mm of fabric and stitch it once. Then stitch the Dacron reinforcement lines - along the dotted lines shown in Figure 1 - onto nine of the ribs. Just stitch on top of the line (the sewing machine should be able to do this); you may have to adjust the tension of the thread at some point (practice this on some leftover fabric). Start at point 1, sew close to the front edge to A, turn the fabric around with the needle still in it and follow the same course, via Point 2 and Point B, to Point 3. Before starting with the major part of the sewing, first hem in 5 mm along the length of both top and bottom layers.

The ribs are then sewn one by one onto the bottom layer of fabric, exactly along the pencil

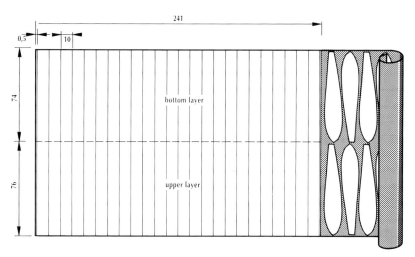

2 *The most economic way to cut the kite out of the fabric.*

3 *An 'exploded view' of the Krypton-S.*

4 *To close the last seam, shove the entire kite into the last cell.*

lines. Start right at Point A, on the edge of the (un-hemmed) bottom layer; make a few back and forth stitches, about 2 cm, so that the front of each rib is firmly attached. Also, make sure the seams of the first and last ribs face inside; all of the other ribs can be sewn with seams either to the right or to the left, depending on which side one starts sewing. After finishing the ribs, each profile should end at the same distance from the edge of the bottom layer. If the difference is more than 1 cm, undo it and try again. However, this does not apply to the first and last ribs at the wing tips because these are much more difficult to sew with the same tolerance.

Attaching the ribs to the upper layer works the same way but requires some skill since the ribs are already attached to the bottom layer. Start with rib 1 right at the edge of the fabric. Here too, have the seams at the tips face inward. Also, make sure the trailing edge is even. To make the last seam face

inward, roll up the kite tightly. Then fold the upper layer to the left and the last rib to the right. Now you have a kite which can easily be sewn and, later, turned inside out with the help of the openings in the front and at the back. Except for the closing hem of the trailing edge, your (first) sparless kite is just about ready. But before you make the hem, first put the kite on a large table and smooth it out completely. Now the (rather uneven) trailing edge can be cut in a straight line, about 1 - 2 cm from the tips of the ribs. The straight section of each profile tip remains unstitched but will - to a certain extent - eventually flatten out when the kite is stitched together. Flatten the first and last ribs and stitch them across so that they protrude towards the outside (air should not be able to escape here).

BRIDLING

Hammer two small nails into a bridle plank: one at 71 cm and one at 68.7 cm. Wrap the line nine

times around the nails as shown - they will become the primary V-lines. Mark them at point 0 and hot-cut them where they touch the nails. With a darning needle, push the longer line through the fabric and around the reinforcement line at Point A. Make an overhand knot - a 'securing knot' - at the end; then make a slip-knot and draw it up to the securing knot (see 'bridle knot' in the chapter on knots). At Point B repeat the same procedure with the shorter end of the line. Then cut and tie end-loops in the 9 so-called 'suspension lines' or 'secondary bridle' according to the measurements given. With a pen, mark the necessary interval points on the thick arc-line. With a strong darning needle push the loops of the suspension lines through the arc-line to their respective places (you may need to use pliers here) and attach them to the arc-line with a larks head. Make an overhand knot at the loose ends, and with a double-sheet bend attach each suspension line to their respect-

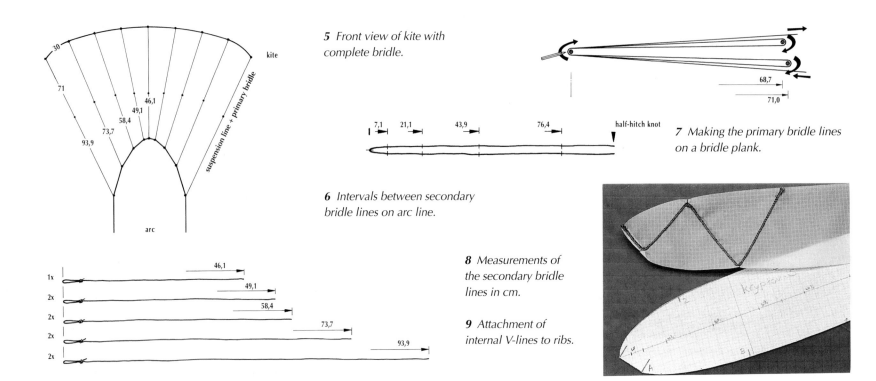

5 *Front view of kite with complete bridle.*

6 *Intervals between secondary bridle lines on arc line.*

7 *Making the primary bridle lines on a bridle plank.*

8 *Measurements of the secondary bridle lines in cm.*

9 *Attachment of internal V-lines to ribs.*

ive V-lines, exactly on the spots you marked previously. Here too, draw the knot up to the securing knot so that no loose ends protrude.

Make overhand knots at the ends of the arc-line and your Krypton-S is ready for launching!

LAUNCHING

Place the kite flat on the ground, at right angles to the wind, with the bridle lines facing up and the air-intakes facing away from the wind. Place some sand on the trailing edge of the kite so it stays on the ground. If there isn't any sand around, an assistant is indispensable. Walk towards the hand grips, pull at the lines carefully until the front of the Krypton-S lifts up and it fills with air. Now give

the kite a controlled tug and take a step back. The kite should now be adequately filled with air and fly straight up. 'Pumping' the kite a few times will open up any remaining stubborn cells.

ADJUSTMENTS

It is easy to check the difference in lengths of the two lines connected to each rib: the line in the front should be 23 mm longer than the line at the back.

If the kite does not fill up and fly well, the bridle is too 'low'. Slide all the sheet bend knots forward so that the lines in the front become slightly shorter and the difference in length of the two lines will decrease.

If the kite is easy to launch but does not pull very well the bridle is too 'high'; you will also find

that with this setting the Krypton-S will collapse in tight turns. Slide the sheet bend knots towards point B; the difference in length of the two lines will now increase.

In order to achieve the ideal tight-turning characteristics, we recommend you to vary the setting of the bridle lines. Try, for example, a difference of 20 mm in the centre of the kite, to 35 mm at the wing tips of the kite.

It is also a good idea to have someone else fly the Krypton-S, so you can observe the kite from different angles. If you happen to see a kink in the otherwise smooth curvature of the kite, you may need to re-adjust the length of one of the suspension lines.

18 SPUTNIK 4

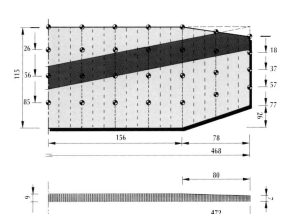

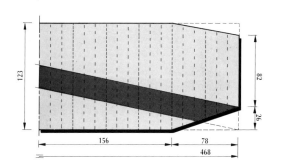

1 Lower skin of Sputnik 4 (5 m²).

2 And the upper skin.

3 Profile of Sputnik 4
with co-ordinates for profiles 1 - 13.

profile co-ordinates Sputnik 4

profiles 1-13		profile 14		profile 15		profile 16		profile 17		profile 18		profile 19	
117 cm		110,5 cm		104 cm		97,5 cm		91 cm		84,5 cm		78 cm	
X	Y	X	Y	X	Y	X	Y	X	Y	X	Y	X	Y
mm	mm	mm	mm	mm	mm	mm	mm	mm	mm	mm	mm	mm	mm
0	0	0	0	0	0	0	0	0	0	0	0	0	0
41	47	38	44	36	42	34	39	32	36	29	34	27	31
83	68	78	64	73	60	69	56	64	53	60	49	55	45
176	87	166	83	157	78	147	73	137	68	127	63	117	58
293	99	277	93	261	88	244	82	228	77	212	71	195	66
410	100	387	94	365	89	342	83	319	78	296	72	273	67
585	95	553	90	520	84	488	79	455	74	423	69	390	63
878	71	829	68	781	64	732	60	683	56	634	52	585	48
1170	35	1105	33	1040	31	975	29	910	27	845	25	780	23

primary bridle Sputnik 4

rows 1-13	row 16	row 19	
113.6 cm	94.7 cm	75.7 cm	a-line
107.5 cm	89.6 cm	71.6 cm	b-line
113.9 cm	94.9 cm	75.9 cm	c-line
128.6 cm	107.1 cm	85.7 cm	d-line

Wingspan	4.68 m
Aspect Ratio	4.24
Surface area	5.17 m²
Weight	800 grams
Wind range	Icarex fabric: 1 - 6 Beaufort
	Carrington fabric: 2 - 8 Beaufort
Control lines	←//→ 150 - 300 kg

MATERIALS

17 m	spinnaker (10 m colour 1 and 7 m colour 2)
60 m	Dacron line, ←//→ 50 kg
45 m	Dacron line, ←//→ 75 kg
4 m	braided line, 3 to 4 mm Ø
5 m	gauze fabric, minimum width 9 cm
1 roll	± 400 m polyester sewing-thread # 60

PREPARATION

This 5 m² Sputnik comes in two versions: a completely rectangular Sputnik - all 37 profiles having the same measurements - or, as in the figure, a Sputnik with tapering wing tips. There is not much difference between the two as far as flight performance is concerned; the one with the tapering wing tips keeps the kite in slightly better shape under difficult circumstances (e.g. turbulent winds). It is up to you whether you want to put a lot of work into making a beautiful kite, or merely whip together a fast and easy, but purely functional 'draught-horse'.

The following construction plans assume that you will be making the Sputnik with tapering wing tips.

CUTTING / DRAWING

Start with the large pieces for the upper and lower skins; all leftover material can be used to make the ribs. To obtain the necessary width of 123 cm from 104 cm (40") material, first cut out two pieces of 468 cm length using the complete width of the fabric (104 cm) of colour no. 1. These pieces are then diagonally cut into two: a 25 cm wide strip of the contrasting colour no. 2 is placed between the two pieces of fabric and sewn together. The alternative to widening the fabric is to add this strip to either side of the material. With a soft pencil, draw the profile lines for the ribs clearly onto both pieces of fabric; mark the positions for the bridle attachments on the bottom layer.

Now the tapering wing tip segments can be cut off. If you want to be precise, leave 7 mm for seam allowances on the sides, but this is negligible on a wing span of 4.68 m. The seams on the gauze and rear edges are included in the measurements. If you want more room for error, widen both the upper and lower skins a few centimetres at their respective trailing edge so that you can always trim off any excess fabric after the kite has been sewn together.

Cut the gauze as per the drawing; for the rectangular version, the entire strip should have a width of 9 cm. You should use wide-meshed gauze of 1 or 2 mm mesh-size. This material is hard to find; ask your local kite store or try an upholstery/drapery store.

PROFILE TEMPLATES

Each rib gets the exact shape of an airfoil profile. In the rectangular Spuntik all ribs are identical, for the tapered wing tips several sizes of templates have to be made. Draw and cut out the profile templates from a sheet of cardboard (approximately 1 mm thick).

First draw a base line indicating the length of the profile; draw the coordinates onto this line according to the table of measurements. A thin fibre-glass rod comes in handy when drawing a smooth curve connecting the coordinates. Use a 2 mm Ø rod of fibre-glass for the nose and a 3 mm Ø rod for the rest of the profile. The measurements of the rib-profiles include approximately 10 mm wide seams.

Cutting out the ribs in a precise way works best by placing the templates on top of the fabric and by hot-cutting the fabric along the contours of the templates with a soldering iron. It is important to keep the grain of the material parallel to the base line and to mark the exact location on the centre of the profile on each rib.

SEWING

When sewing sparless kites such as this Sputnik, extra attention must be paid to the quality of the seams; proper doubling-up of the stitches at the beginning and at the end of the seams is necessary. When sewing the ribs, take particular care when the thread in the bobbin runs out. Irrevocable damage can be done to the kite if the stitches of the profiles come loose in flight.

Important: Before actually sewing the kite, it is advisable to reinforce the lower skin of the areas where the bridle attachment points are cut out; glue and stitch 4 x 4 cm squares folded diagonally onto each of these points.

1 Attach the gauze to the bottom skin. By folding 7 mm of the spinnaker over the gauze you prevent it sliding away from the fabric when sewing.

2 Fold the gauze over and sew a second seam. This seam will have a 'nice' spinnaker side and a 'plain' gauze side. The upper skin is attached to the other side of the gauze in the same manner. Make sure the 'nice' seam appears on the same side; this will, of course, become the kite's outer part. The pencil marks should now be on the inside of the kite.

3 The next step involves stitching the ribs onto the lower skin. Place the 'centre of profile' mark of the rib exactly against the stitches of the upper skin/gauze-seam and sew the rib onto the gauze and bottom skin, meticulously following the pencil lines. Material with a lighter colour now has an advantage. It does not really matter whether you start from the

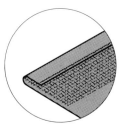

4 Attachment gauze on lower skin.

5 Fold back and sew a second time.

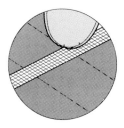

6 Sewing a profile.

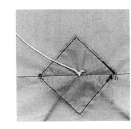

7 Reinforcements on lower skin.

left or right side of the kite - either way you are going to have to push a mountain of fabric through the sewing machine. Do pay attention to the first and last ribs as their seams need to be turned inside.

4 Now that all the ribs have been sewn to the lower skin, the reinforcement cords for the bridle attachments can be sewn onto every third rib. Practice this stitch work of cord onto spinnaker on some test strips - adjustments often have to be made on the thread-tension of your sewing machine in order to get the correct stitch. Use Dacron line with a breaking strength of 75 kg. If your sewing machine has some accessory pressure feet, file a groove on the bottom of one of them; this groove will

help guide the cord on the fabric along the direction desired.

Start at Point 1, as shown in Figure 3. The exact location of this point is not definite; you can determine it yourself as long as the cord crosses diagonally and comes out exactly at Point D. This point is marked on the bottom skin. Keep sewing until the thread has gone through the bottom layer at Point D once (on attaching the bridle, this point can easily be found again). Stop sewing, turn the fabric around and sew back to point 2. The exact location of Point 2 is arbitrary; at that point, turn the fabric around again and try as precisely as possible, to find your way to Point C. In this manner, work your way to Point 5; the entire procedure is repeated on the other 12 profiles with bridle-attachments.

5   Now all the profiles can be sewn onto the upper skin, starting at the mark on the nose, where the sewing of the lower skin began. The small vertical part at the end of each profile does not get stitched.

The last small profile which closes off the interior gets the same treatment. With the seam facing the outside, the larger part of the kite - which is inside out - ends up in the last cell. After completing the last profile, the somewhat crumpled kite is pulled out of that cell.

6   The way the profiles end at the trailing edge will show just how precisely and consistently you made the kite. If they all end up at an equal distance - perfect! Differences of more than 1 cm will cause parts of the trailing edge to flare up or down once the kite is airborne. It is adviseable to unpick any rib that is too far off the mark. The easiest way to finish off the edges is to simply stitch the top and bottom skins together 1 cm from where the profiles end and then hot-cut the

remaining fabric off. The first and last profile can be flattened to the outside, and stitched closed, so that no air can escape.

BRIDLING
The bridle of Sputnik 4 comprises three different sections.

Primary bridle lines
Each rib with a bridle is supported by four bridle lines coming together in one knot - this is called the primary bridle point. The location of this bridle point determines - for 90 per cent - the flight performance of the Sputnik, so work carefully.

On each rib the first line together with the second line are formed by one V-line; the third and fourth lines are made the same way. Cut and mark the 50 kg Dacron line as per the figure. Applying little stripes in different colours helps prevent mistakes. To make the lines exactly the same length, use a bridle plank (See Chapter on 'The Working Area').

The lines are now attached to the kite with a darning needle. Thread the needle with the V-line and push the needle through the bottom skin, around the internal reinforcement cord and through the rib back out. At the end of the line make an overhand knot (Cf. Appendix 'Knots') and tie the line with a bridle-hitch.

Cut 13 pieces of 75 kg Dacron line, each 15 cm long. Place overhand knots at all ends; the ends are attached to the main V-lines by means of a sheet bend. This creates 13 small V-lines.

Arch bridle
Mark the middle of the thick braided line. Fold it over and mark the secondary bridle line spacings onto this line. Place overhand knots at the ends.

Secondary bridle lines
These lines connect the primary lines to the arch. The length of the secondary lines should include the loop with the overhand knot at one end; the bridle plank comes in handy here too. Use 75 kg line for the secondary lines.

Thread a small part of the loop through the eye of a sturdy darning needle and push the entire line through the arch at the appropriate point. Remove the needle and attach the secondary line to the arch with a lark's head. Attach all the secondary lines to the arch in this way and place overhand knots on any remaining loose ends.

Lastly, attach the ends of the secondary lines to the middle of the small V-lines of the primary bridle lines with a sheet bend.

TEST FLYING AND ADJUSTMENTS
As we mentioned earlier, the location of the bridle point is extremely important. On Sputnik 4, the bridle point is located perpendicular to the profile-base line at a distance equal to the length of the profile and 18 per cent from the nose. If the length of the profile is 100 cm, for example, then it is 18 cm from the nose and 100 cm from the kite's central axis. If the knots are placed properly, your Sputnik will fly perfectly in all wind conditions, without your having to make any further adjustments.

In practice, however, no one sews and knots a kite the same way. So if your Sputnik does not fly well, adjust the bridles according to the following rules.

BASIC ADJUSTMENTS
Conduct the following adjustments in stable winds between 2 and 4 Beaufort.

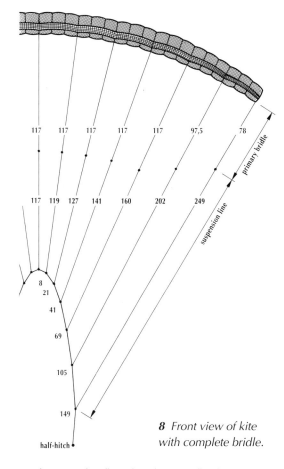

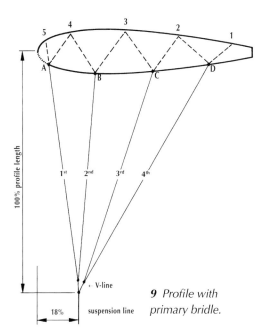

8 Front view of kite with complete bridle.

9 Profile with primary bridle.

10 This Sputnik 3 has winglets to reduce pressure-loss on the wing tips. The bubble at the ninth rib from the top indicates a tear on the inside.

1 The Sputnik inflates but does not fly, does not rise or does not fly well.
Cause: the bridle is set too low; the bridle point must be moved towards the nose.
Undo the sheet bend on the first V-line and shorten the 1st bridle line by approximately 1 cm.

2 The Sputnik flies well but after a short while the nose collapses in the direction of its pilot.
Cause: the bridle is set too high; the bridle point must be moved away from the nose.

Undo the foremost sheet bend knot and lengthen bridle line 1 by approximately 1 cm.

FINE-TUNING

After the basic adjustments have been completed, the Sputnik should be alright. But if you want optimum performance, you can fine-tune the kite in the following ways:

1 Fly horizontally, low over the ground. If the Sputnik tends to fly somewhat at an angle (like a crab) with the lower wing tip leading its path, the bridle is still set somewhat too low. Shorten the first row of bridle lines by a few millimetres.

2 Park the Sputnik above your head and 'pump' the kite (tug both lines hard) a few times. If the nose collapses forward, then the Sputnik is bridled a bit too high. Lengthen the first row of bridle lines by a few millimetres.

If you still cannot find the optimum bridle position, try lengthening the lines in the fourth row by 1 cm. Now repeat the above fine-tuning procedure again.

VARIATIONS

The 5 m² Sputnik 4 is the ideal kite to buggy-race in medium (between 2.5 and 5 Beaufort) winds. We have built smaller and much larger variations for different circumstances.

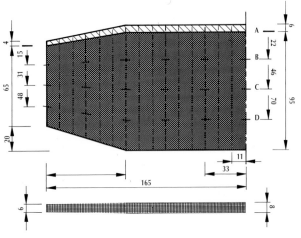

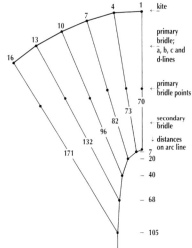

kite

primary bridle; a, b, c and d-lines

primary bridle points

secondary bridle

distances on arc line

11 *2.8 m² Sputnik 4.*

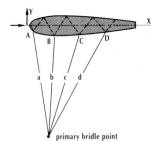

12 *Profile with primary bridle.*

primary bridle point

13 *Front view of the bridle. Unlike the 5 m² Sputnik, this small version has only 11 secondary bridle lines.*

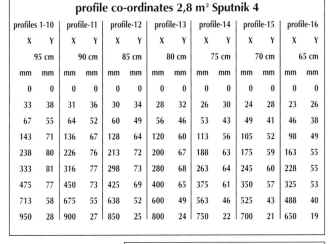

profile co-ordinates 2,8 m² Sputnik 4													
profiles 1-10		profile-11		profile-12		profile-13		profile-14		profile-15		profile-16	
X	Y	X	Y	X	Y	X	Y	X	Y	X	Y	X	Y
95 cm		90 cm		85 cm		80 cm		75 cm		70 cm		65 cm	
mm	mm	mm	mm	mm	mm	mm	mm	mm	mm	mm	mm	mm	mm
0	0	0	0	0	0	0	0	0	0	0	0	0	0
33	38	31	36	30	34	28	32	26	30	24	28	23	26
67	55	64	52	60	49	56	46	53	43	49	41	46	38
143	71	136	67	128	64	120	60	113	56	105	52	98	49
238	80	226	76	213	72	200	67	188	63	175	59	163	55
333	81	316	77	298	73	280	68	263	64	245	60	228	55
475	77	450	73	425	69	400	65	375	61	350	57	325	53
713	58	675	55	638	52	600	49	563	46	525	43	488	40
950	28	900	27	850	25	800	24	750	22	700	21	650	19

primary bridle 2,8 m² Sputnik 4			
rows 1-10	row 13	row 16	
92.2 cm	76.9 cm	61.5 cm	a-line
87.3 cm	72.7 cm	58.2 cm	b-line
92.4 cm	77.0 cm	61.6 cm	c-line
104.4 cm	87.0 cm	69.6 cm	d-line

2,8 M² SPUTNIK 4

Wingspan	3.3 m
Aspect Ratio	3.9
Surface area	2.8 m²
Weight	450 g (P 38 polyester fabric)
Wind range	1 - 8 Beaufort
Control lines	←//→ 150 - 300 kg

MATERIALS

12 m	spinnaker nylon or spinnaker polyester
50 m	Dacron line, ←//→ 50 kg
40 m	Dacron line, ←//→ 75 kg
3 m	braided line, 3 to 4 mm Ø
4 m	gauze fabric, minimum width 8 cm

These measurements allow you to use the width of the fabric optimally (min. width: 104 cm); the lift and speed of this kite make it an ideal kite for buggy-sailing in strong winds (5 Beaufort and above). The low Aspect Ratio makes this kite more manoeuvrable and reduces its tendency to collapse, while the loss of aerodynamic efficiency has no influence on the kite when it is flown in strong winds - in fact this kite is meant to fly in such winds.

The drawing shows one half of the kite with the measurements of the lower skin; the strip at the leading edge indicates how much larger the upper skin is. Besides the profile coordinates, all measurements are in centimetres.

10 M² SPUTNIK 4

Wingspan	6.12 m
Aspect Ratio	3.7
Surface area	10 m²
Weight	1400 g (P 31 polyester fabric)
Wind range	1 - 4 Beaufort
Control lines	←//→ 150 - 300 kg

MATERIALS

40 m	spinnaker nylon or spinnaker polyester
90 m	Dacron line, ←//→ 50 kg
60 m	Dacron line, ←//→ 75 kg
6 m	braided line, 3 to 4 mm Ø
7 m	gauze fabric, minimum width 10cm

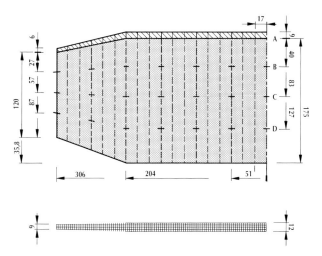

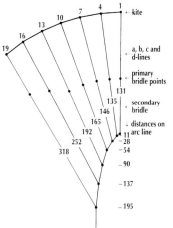

profile co-ordinates 10 m² Sputnik 4													
profiles 1-13		profile 14		profile 15		profile 16		profile 17		profile 18		profile 19	
175	cm	166	cm	157	cm	147	cm	138	cm	129	cm	120	cm
X	Y	X	Y	X	Y	X	Y	X	Y	X	Y	X	Y
mm	mm	mm	mm	mm	mm	mm	mm	mm	mm	mm	mm	mm	mm
0	0	0	0	0	0	0	0	0	0	0	0	0	0
61	70	58	66	54	63	51	59	48	55	45	52	42	48
123	101	117	96	110	91	104	85	98	80	91	75	85	70
263	131	249	124	236	117	222	110	208	103	194	97	181	90
438	147	415	140	392	132	369	124	346	117	324	109	301	101
613	149	581	141	549	134	517	126	485	118	453	110	421	102
874	142	829	134	783	127	737	120	691	112	646	105	600	97
1312	107	1244	101	1175	96	1107	90	1038	84	969	79	901	73
1750	52	1657	49	1566	46	1474	44	1383	41	1291	38	1200	35

14 The largest Sputnik in this book: more than 10 m².

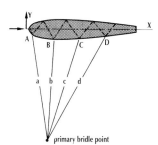

15 Profile of the 10 m² with primary bridle.

16 This large Sputnik also has 13 secondary bridle lines.

This giant is meant for buggying in light winds (1 or 2 Beaufort); in addition, kites with such a large surface area are necessary to reach high speeds on boats and water skis.

This kite too has been given a low Aspect Ratio on purpose: despite its large size, this kite remains easy to manoeuvre.

What you see is only one half of the kite with the measurements of the lower skin; the extra strip indicates the upper skin. Besides the profile co-ordinates, all measurements are in centimetres.

17 To launch the Sputnik: face the bridle into the wind, place the kite on its back and pile some sand on the lower edge.

primary bridle 10 m² Sputnik 4			
rows 1-13	row 16	row 19	
169.8 cm	143.1 cm	116.5 cm	a-line
160.6 cm	135.4 cm	110.2 cm	b-line
170.2 cm	143.5 cm	116.8 cm	c-line
192.1 cm	162.0 cm	131.8 cm	d-line

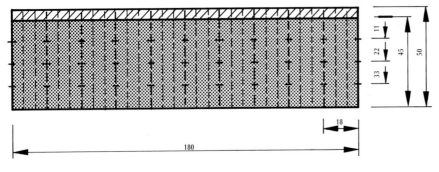

18 0.8 m² Sputnik 3.

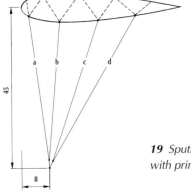

19 Sputnik 3 profile with primary bridle.

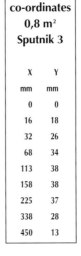

profile co-ordinates 0,8 m² Sputnik 3	
X	Y
mm	mm
0	0
16	18
32	26
68	34
113	38
158	38
225	37
338	28
450	13

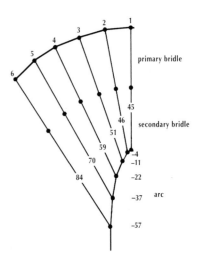

20 Front view of 0.8 m² bridle.

And finally, the smallest Sputnik we have been able to fly: the miniature Sputnik of only 0.8 m². This kite differs from the larger Sputniks in two ways: it has a rectangular shape (rather than a tapering one) and the ribs are pointed (the Sputnik 3 profile).

0,8 M² SPUTNIK 3

Wingspan	1.8 m
Aspect Ratio	4
Surface area	0.81 m²
Weight	140 grams
Wind range	2 - 8 Beaufort
Control lines	←//→ 25 - 100 kg

MATERIALS

3.5 m	spinnaker polyester P 31
25 m	Spectra / Dyneema, ←//→ 20 kg
25 m	Spectra / Dyneema, ←//→ 50 kg
2 m	braided line, 3 to 4 mm Ø
2 m	gauze fabric, minimum width 5 cm

primary bridle 0,8 m² Sputnik 3	
a-line	43.7 cm
b-line	41.3 cm
c-line	43.8 cm
d-line	49.4 cm

EXTRA TIPS

A sparless kite is handled differently from a stunt-delta kite. The fact that a sparless kite has no frame to break certainly does not mean it is unbreakable. When flying a sparless kite, the most important thing to care about is when it crashes to the ground or onto the water at full speed. The gauze opening can be blocked,

21 The bridle lines are tied together in a parachute knot.

preventing air from escaping, and as a result, the flying speed is converted into an air-pressure 'explosion' which can be large enough to snap the seams or even tear open the kite. To land the kite safely, manoeuvre the kite to the edge of the wind window, either to the left or right.

22 Winglets reduce the loss of pressure on wing tips. (C stands for profile length.)

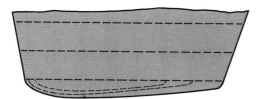

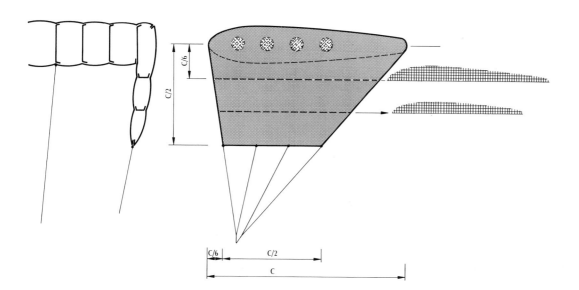

23 The stunt kite which failed to become the world's largest. This kite (made by Dominique Scholtes and the authors) is indeed enormous (20 metres wingspan, almost 100 m² surface area) but the required loops must still be realised.

along the entire span of the kite. Let the kite inflate, brace yourself for the force to come and give the grips an easy tug, just enough to allow the Sputnik to lift up;
- in 4 Beaufort winds or more, it is advisable to launch large kites such as Sputnik 4 from the edge of the wind window instead of the centre in order to prevent sudden uncontrollable 'explosions' of force from dragging you away.

WINGLETS

Winglets are small fins located at the wingtips. In theory, they reduce the pressure-loss via the wingtips.

The drawing shows the construction of a Sputnik winglet. The same construction can be used for other sparless kite types. Profiles for these winglets are shaped the same as the rest of the kite but are cut in half. Both ends of the wing are thus elongated by a half-profile. The winglets consist of an 'inner' and 'outer' layer. The former is flat; the latter follows the contour of the profile and should be given an allowance of 5 per cent before curring. The winglets are inflated by air which enters the main wing via the tip profiles.

Preferably, have someone hold down the kite once it has landed so that it does not take off again. This can be especially dangerous when it happens while you are rolling up the lines - the kite will take off and, because you can no longer control it, will crash to the ground at full speed (the result of which has been mentioned above). Not only can the kite be damaged, it can also sweep bystanders off their feet in the process.

If you have to launch a Sputnik without help, go about it as follows:

- place the kite belly-up with the gauze opening facing downwind and the bridle lines facing upwind;
- put some sand or other small objects onto the trailing edge of the kite to keep it on the ground and bring the wing tips forward into the wind, banana-shaping the kite;
- check the bridle lines for hitches or knots, then attach the control lines to the bridle using lark's head knots;
- walk towards your grips and tension the control lines. The gauze edge should rise evenly

19 PIRAÑA

Wingspan	4.54 m
Surface area	4 m²
Weight	850 g
Wind range	Beaufort 2-4
Control lines	←//→ 150 - 200 kg

MATERIALS

30 m	spinnaker polyester, Icarex P-31
10 m	gauze, 10 cm wide
75 m	Dacron bridle line, ←//→ 50 kg
50 m	Dacron bridle line, ←//→ 75 kg
4 m	braided line, 3 - 4 mm Ø

PREPARATIONS

The above list of materials may appear scant for such a large and complicated kite - obviously it would be more fun to make the various parts of the Piraña (e.g. the body, wings, tail, fin, eyes, teeth, mouth, scales and the patterns on the wings) in different colours. The choice is yours, however; it is also up to you to figure out how much fabric you need if you decide to use several

1 A rough sketch of the Escher etching, our source of inspiration.

colours. The above list gives you a general idea as to how much it is going to cost you in terms of material.

Because of its bright colours, our Piraña is more of a caricature of the fish rather than a real-life resemblance. The name came to us one day as we were flying a prototype with a 9-metre wingspan; the fish crashed on top of an unsuspecting by-stander, gobbling her up with its enormous mouth in a single, well-aimed bite. The fish in one of M.C. Escher's etchings (which inspired us to make this kite) has a smiling mouth, closed shut; as a kite, Escher's fish would have been difficult to inflate! By giving the Piraña a sinister grin, we made it possible for the air to

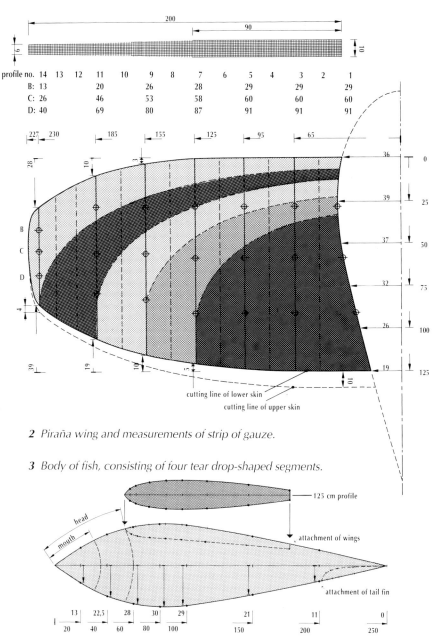

2 Piraña wing and measurements of strip of gauze.

3 Body of fish, consisting of four tear drop-shaped segments.

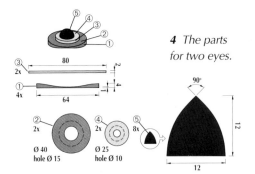

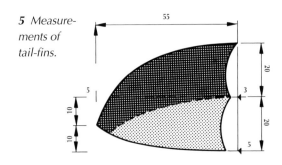

4 The parts for two eyes.

5 Measurements of tail-fins.

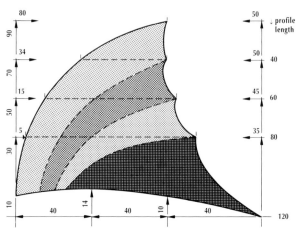

6 Measurements of dorsal fin.

7 The (largest) profile of the dorsal fin. This one is not cut out; it is drawn onto the body of the Piraña.

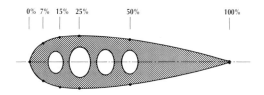

flow freely into the kite.

The attractive point to the kite's design is that a few, slight modifications can easily transform the shape into an aeroplane, whale, spaceship, wasp, etc.

There are no step-by-step instructions for this kite; we assume you have already made a Krypton and a Sputnik. We do, however, provide you with the appropriate order in which the various parts of the kite are sewn together so that you do not end up like a present-day Jonah, locked up with your sewing machine in the belly of a fish.

DRAWING AND CUTTING

The Piraña is made from a number of similarly shaped segments so it is worth making cardboard templates first. There are no seam allowances in any of the drawings - they are your responsibility. An exception, however, are the ribs: these can be cut out exactly according to the given profile coordinates. Many ribs are the same as those of a standard Sputnik, so there is a good chance you already have most of the templates. The measurements and shape for one wing-half are provided for the lower skin. This template can also be used for the upper skin by adding a strip to the trailing edge as shown in the shaded area in the drawing.

The dorsal and tail fins are very thick; this gives them more volume and allows them to maintain their shape without any support. The air for inflating the fins enters through the body, via the mouth and venting holes located in the ribs. To prevent the fabric around the holes from fraying, it is advisable to cover the holes with gauze. The tail-fin pattern needs to be cut four times, the dorsal-fin twice.

The body consists of four segments, each shaped like an elongated drop of water; the template for these can be cut into smaller segments. Different colours for each segment give the fish an accentuated head and suggest scales on the body. The opening of the mouth is made by cutting away the indicated parts of the two segments as shown in the drawing.

The eyes consist of several layers; these layers have holes in them which allow air to flow in. The measurements for all parts have been provided. Cut out the eight, orange-peel shaped pieces, two small circles, two large circles, two straight edges and the four concave edges.

ORDER OF CONSTRUCTION

1 Sew both wings together like two Sputnik halves; include the tapering gauze strip and the zigzag-shaped reinforcement lines on the ribs where the bridle will eventually come. There is no rib where the wings are later attached to the body. The last 5 cm of the wing tips do not have ribs either; they are simply hemmed. You can leave the seam on the trailing edge open for the time being.

2 Sew the dorsal-fin and one of the two tail-fins together without the usual gauze fabric on the leading edge; instead, make holes in the profiles so that the air can flow through, or make the profiles completely from gauze.

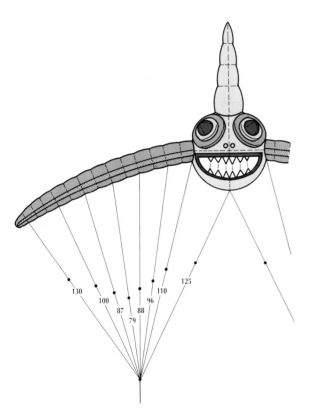

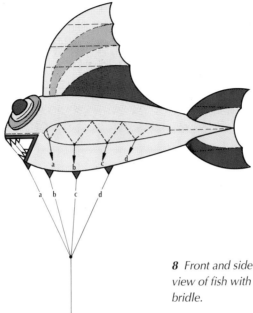

8 *Front and side view of fish with bridle.*

7 Connect the fin and tail-fin and close off their trailing edges.

8 Sew on the remaining body pieces (with the mouth openings) onto both sides.

9 Mark the outlines of the 125 cm profiles onto both sides of the body. Mark the spot where the zigzag reinforcement line should come; sew the line on.

10 Now it is time to attach the wings. The method of sewing is the same as that of sewing ribs in the wings. Start from the nose at the gauze and stitch first the upper and then the lower skin, from front to back. Now the trailing edge of both wings can be finished off.

11 The seam along the belly is the closing seam. Since the bottom part of the tail fin is attached on top of this seam it means this fin has to be sewn as two separate halves first. Mark both (half-) profile lines onto the body and cut out a few ventilation holes (add gauze). Now sew a tail-fin panel onto each side of the body. Close the entire body and sew on Dacron reinforcement for the bridle attachments. Finish off the tail-fin in the usual manner.

12 Finish off the opening of the mouth with a 5 cm strip of red spinnaker. Hem in the strip and thread a piece of cord through it so that the size of the opening can be adjusted.

13 Finishing touch: create a set of teeth to your own design and attach to the inside of the mouth. A piece of cord connecting the teeth on the upper jaw to the ones on the lower jaw will help retain their shape.

3 The body consists of four segments, each of which can be multi-coloured, depending on taste. Do not sew these pieces together yet.

4 For the eyes, sew the four quarter-pieces together so that you have a semi-sphere. Sew this bubble onto the small circle. Stitch the straight narrow edge to it, then sew the entire thing onto the large circle. Sew the two concave edges to the large circle. Work accurately or the circles will not come out evenly. It helps to place marks along the circle, like a dial with stripes for 12, 3, 6,

and 9 o'clock. This leaves room for corrections while sewing; a larger curve can be used when there is too much fabric, a tighter curve when there is too little.

5 The concave edges of the eyes keep the circles flat after they have been attached to the curved body. Align the narrow part of the edge along the central axis of the fish while sewing; the widest part of the edge now touches both sides of the body segment. Do not forget to cut vent-holes in the body segment so that air flows into the eyes.

6 The two body segments with the eyes can now be stitched together. The profile-shaped attachment for the back and tail-fin can also be marked on the material. Cut out ventilation holes here too; it is advisable to use gauze reinforcement.

BRIDLE

Follow the primary bridle instructions for the Sputnik, but use the measurements given on the next page. The bridling and angle of attack are

profile measurements																	
(X is plotted horizontally, Y is plotted above and below the corresponding x co-ordinate)																	
1 t/m 6		7		8		9		10		11		12		13		14	
125 cm		120 cm		115 cm		110 cm		105 cm		95 cm		85 cm		70cm		55 cm	
X	Y	X	Y	X	Y	X	Y	X	Y	X	Y	X	Y	X	Y	X	Y
0	0	0	0	0	0	0	0	0	0	0	0	0	0	0	0	0	0
43	50	42	48	40	46	38	44	37	42	33	38	30	34	24	28	19	22
88	72	85	70	81	67	78	64	74	61	67	55	60	49	49	41	39	32
188	93	181	90	173	86	166	82	158	79	143	71	128	64	105	52	83	41
313	105	301	101	288	97	276	93	263	88	238	80	213	72	175	59	138	46
438	107	421	102	403	98	386	94	368	90	333	81	298	73	245	60	193	47
625	101	600	97	575	93	550	89	525	85	475	77	425	69	350	57	275	45
938	76	901	73	863	70	826	67	788	64	713	58	638	52	525	43	413	34
1250	37	1200	35	1150	34	1100	32	1050	31	950	28	850	25	700	21	550	16

9 *Side view of Piraña. The dorsal and tail-fin retain their shape through internal pressure.*

length primary bridle:								
	rump	profile-1	profile-3	profile-5	profile-7	profile-9	profile-11	profile-14
a-line	109 cm	120 cm	120 cm	120 cm	120 cm	106 cm	91 cm	53 cm
b-line	88 cm	116 cm	116 cm	116 cm	116 cm	102 cm	88 cm	51 cm
c-line	82 cm	125 cm	125 cm	125 cm	125 cm	110 cm	95 cm	55 cm
d-line	94 cm	143 cm	143 cm	143 cm	143 cm	126 cm	109 cm	63 cm

fin profile measurements: (X horizontal, Y vertical)											
	40 cm		50 cm		60 cm		80 cm		120 cm		
	X	Y	X	Y	X	Y	X	Y	X	Y	
0%	0	0	0	0	0	0	0	0	0	0	0%
7%	3	4	4	5	4	4	6	7	8	11	7%
15%	6	5	8	6	9	7	12	9	18	14	15%
25%	10	5	13	6	15	8	20	10	30	15	25%
50%	20	4	25	5	30	7	40	9	60	13	50%
100%	40	1	50	1	60	1	80	1	120	1	100%

Profiles 120 cm and 50 cm are not cut out, but are drawn onto the Piraña body.

10 *Detail of eye. Each eye consists of four round segments.*

somewhat different on this kite because the body of the fish strongly influences the way the kite flies. Due to all the additional drag the Piraña flies much slower than a Sputnik, the reason the bridle-point is set much higher than normal: 10 per cent instead of 18 per cent from the nose of the profile. If you have problems controlling the Piraña, contrary to what you would expect, the bridle needs to be set higher and not lower.

VARIATIONS

This kite can be modified into various shapes, but remember the more bulges you give the kite the harder it is for it to function as a stunt kite. With the Piraña we are close to the limit; nevertheless, buggying is possible with a 4 m² surface area Piraña!

Creating kites with an equally wild or even wilder shape than the Piraña will always be an interesting challenge, even if the kite turns out to be a static rather than manoeuvrable one.

20 QUADRIPHANT

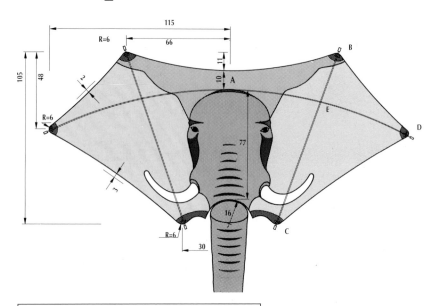

1 Quadriphant measurements.

Wingspan	2.5 m
Surface area	1.5 m²
Weight	400 g
Wind range	1.5 - 5 Beaufort
Control lines	←//→ 50-75 kg, 20 - 35 metre length.

MATERIALS

4 pcs	125 cm carbon-fibre tube 8 mm Ø
2.5 m	spinnaker, colour for ears (1)
2 m	spinnaker, colour for head and snout (2)
0.2 m	spinnaker, colour for wrinkles etc. (3)
0.2 m	spinnaker, white for tusks
2 m	Dacron 10 cm wide, preferably colour (1)
1.5 m	bungee cord 4 mm Ø
6 pcs	nylon end caps with holes 8 mm Ø
14 pcs	eyelets 5 mm Ø
1 pc	8 mm Ø connector
8 m	bias edge tape, black
30 cm	Velcro, 30 mm wide
4 pcs	bridle clips ←//→ 75 kg
7.5 m	bridle line ←//→ 75 kg

TEMPLATES

In order to attain a symmetrical result it is necessary to make a template. You need a sheet of cardboard or thick paper half the size of the kite, at least 105 x 115 cm. Transfer the measurements of the drawing onto the template. You can draw in the outline and the shape of the head and other details by hand or by transferring each point by enlarging the drawing twenty-five times. This can be done by placing transparent graph paper over the drawing; each millimetre equals 2.5 centimetre on the template.

Connect the points in a flowing line; this can be done by hand or with the help of a small flexible glass-fibre rod.

COLOURS

You will only create a realistic looking elephant if you choose the correct colour combinations. A light colour for the base, on top of this a slightly darker tint for the head, and the darkest tint over the first two layers to accentuate eyebrows, cheeks and wrinkles. The colours can range from light to dark grey but also, for example, light pink for the ears, dark pink for the head and maroon for the details. To give the upper rim of the ears a

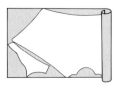

2 Various segments on the fabric.

slightly different shade of colour, an extra layer of the same colour is added.

CUTTING

First draw a perfectly vertical line across the centre of the fabric. Place the template along this line so that Points B and C fit within the fabric. Do not worry if the fabric is slightly (a few centimetres) too narrow; reinforcement material will eventually overlap the missing edges. Cut out this half of the Quadriphant and turn the template over for the other half. Once the outline is cut the contours of the head and the upper sections of the ears are drawn onto the template and cut out. The remaining material from the first fabric is enough to make the double layer used to outline the tips of the ears. The head is then cut out from the slightly darker fabric.

Finally, cut out the eyebrows, cheeks and wrinkles from the template. You now have the appropriate shape of these parts as well as the negative template to trace onto the fabric where the various sections need to be stitched. The corners B, C and D are also cut out of the template - they will be used as small templates for the Dacron reinforcements. For every corner, cut out two pieces of Dacron as the reinforcements will be placed on the front as well as the back of the kite.

Only reinforcement Piece A is cut out once and has the same shape as the bump on the forehead; later it will be stitched onto the back of the kite to

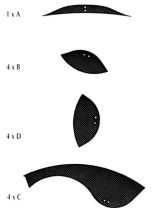

1 x A

4 x B

4 x D

4 x C

3 *Dacron reinforcement pieces.*

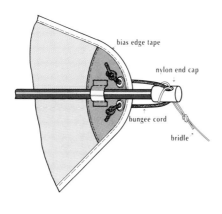

bias edge tape

nylon end cap

bungee cord

bridle

4 *Construction of wing tip with horizontal spreader and bridle.*

prevent a difference in colour.

The only parts which are not cut out of the template are the tusks because you may want to vary their shape with every new kite that you eventually make. The tusks are therefore drawn directly onto the white spinnaker and cut out. It is advisable to tape all the small template pieces together once you are finished so that no section will be missed for making a second Quadriphant later on.

The eyes are cut out from leftover dark blue or black fabric.

The snout consists of 6 pieces which, when laid out vertically side by side, should add up to the exact width of the fabric.

THE HEAD

First the accentuations (cheeks, eyebrows, wrinkles etc) are drawn onto the head, glued and stitched. For all glue work use a type which does not cause spots to appear, preferably a spray glue as used in

5 *The snout consists of six segments.*

photography because it is almost transparent. Use spray cans with ozone-friendly propellants (a good alternative to using glue is the method of hot-tacking fabrics together, see page 96). Glue the head and the two upper sections of the ears onto the large piece of fabric and then stitch. Then come the tusks which are double-stitched onto the fabric because the fabric at the back will later be cut away. If you do not do this, the tusks will barely be visible once the kite is airborne.

THE SNOUT

On the widest top section a few wrinkles are stitched on first. Then both curved sides of the snout opening are hemmed with bias edge tape and the

three parts of the front and back are stitched together to form a long front and back side.

Place the 'fair' sides on top of each other and sew the edges from the wide part down to the narrow part. If necessary, the tip of the snout can be cut straight in order to correct any asymmetrical stitching and then be stitched closed. Now you can turn the snout inside out. A strip of Velcro must be stitched to the curved rear edge. In order to retain a rounded shape, the Velcro is divided into several short strips and sewn on; any protruding parts are cut away later to round off the edge.

FINISHING TOUCH

First, all the reinforcements are stitched onto the corners. The double Dacron serves not only for extra strength but also supports the rounded corners which gives the elephant a more natural look than sharp corners would. On the back of Corner D a loop of double-folded Dacron is stitched on to keep the cross spar in place. The kite is finished off with pre-folded bias edge tape This is probably the most tricky stitching of the entire kite as the turns are rather tight for a good, proper finishing. Lastly, Velcro is sewn onto the bottom part of the head onto which the snout is attached.

FRAME

The cross spar consists of two 125 cm long RCF 8 mm rods with a connector in the middle. To prevent the rods from breaking along the sides of this connector, glue 5 cm pieces of 6 mm Ø glass- or carbon-fibre rods into the ends of the 8 mm carbon-fibre rods. The spines are sawn off at 117 cm. Nylon end caps of 8 mm Ø are attached to the ends of all six frame rods. Do not use cheap, soft

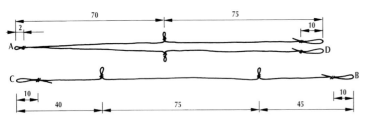

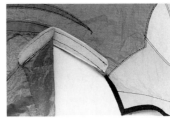

6 Measurements of bridle.

7 The snout is attached to the head with Velcro.

plastic split caps because these will wear out or break in no time at all.

Cut 9 pieces of 15 cm long bungee cords and melt the ends so that they won't fray. To fasten the bungee cord, pierce two holes - 1 cm from the edge and 2 cm from each other - at all the corners. Melting the holes out with a red-hot nail prevents them from tearing; better yet, punch metal eyelets into the holes.

At each corner push the bungee cord through the end cap, then push each of the cord ends through the holes in the Dacron and, finally, make an overhand securing knot. If the rods are now pushed into the plastic caps, the cross spar should tension precisely; if need be, adjust the tension of the cord accordingly or shorten the rods slightly. Now the frame is attached to the fabric at Point A with a 15 cm piece of bungee cord. Use the last two pieces of cord on Point E to connect the spine to the cross spar.

BRIDLE

The bridle consists of a long line running parallel to the cross spar and two shorter lines parallel to each spine.

Knot the lines as illustrated, with long loops at

the ends and short loops for the bridle clips and for the central attachment. The clips have a fixed place, in contrast to the adjustable bridle clips of dual line kites.

Before attaching the bungee cord to the kite, unfasten the cord at Point A, push it through the loop and attach it again. Push the bridle loop through the holes in the nylon end caps at the corners - where the bungee cord has also been pushed through - then place the loop around the cap. This is enough. If necessary, use a 'spleever' to pull the loop through the hole next to the bungee cord.

TIPS

The Quadriphant flies with lines of equal length. Use, if possible, the specially bent quad-line hand grips. Because of the relatively long spines, the deflection of standard hand grips is inadequate, particularly in light wind conditions. In Appendix II we provide a description of how to make special elongated quad-line hand grips which will give you optimum control over the Quadriphant.

Despite its unusual shape, this model is easy to fly, even for the beginner quad-line flier. With similar contours, other true-to-life shapes such as bats and birds of prey are possible.

As with most quad-line kites, it is handy if the frame can be replaced quickly. In light winds, for example, you can use a different frame consisting

of thin High Modulus carbon-fibre rods. The VII-ply-Skyshark rods seem perfect for this purpose. The measurements of the frame are such that three lengths of 82.5 cm are the exact length for the cross spar and 1.5 times 82.5 cm for each spine. The somewhat wide fit into the 8 mm plastic caps is no problem. And if you also choose 1/2 oz lightweight spinnaker fabric, your Quadriphant will glide in the sky even in the slightest of breezes.

'TACKING'

If you want to sew several layers of fabric together, it is better to 'tack' them together first. This is done as follows: take a mini-soldering iron (10 - 25 Watt) with a very fine point and pierce the fabrics along the line you want to sew at 3 - 5 mm intervals. The trail of 'spot-welding' will keep the fabrics together. Now you can sew the fabrics together without the fear of wrinkles developing in the process.

This method is also used in the art of appliqué where two layers of fabric with different colours are tacked and sewn together along the contours of a given design. The top colour is then cut out (with the help of small scissors), leaving only the bottom colour exposed.

I DIKE DIAPER

The Dike Diaper, an invention of Cees van Hengel from the Netherlands, is a square piece of gauze attached to the kite's bridle between the control lines. This diaper-shaped piece of fabric acts as a kind of air brake and helps reduce the kite's speed in strong winds. It also reduces the kite's pull and therefore the risk of frame-damage. At the same time, it allows the flyer to maintain proper control over the kite. It was the Dutch team 'Dike Hoppers' that used this droll piece of fabric on their kites first, hence its name.

The Dike Diaper's size depends on the kite's size as well as the strength of the wind, while its length depends on the distance between the two bridle clips. The measurements should be such that the diaper billows in flight; fabric should be 10 - 15 per cent wider than the distance between the bridle clips.

The height of the diaper determines the amount of drag the kite experiences and thus the speed and pull of the kite. If you increase its height, the kite flies slower. The height of the diaper is usually between 8 and 15 cm.

By making several diapers of various sizes, you can fly the same kite in different wind conditions while retaining the same power.

The construction of the diaper is simple. Decide on its size and cut out a piece of gauze accordingly. Depending on the type of gauze material you use, you may have to give the diaper a double layer. Stitch a strong hem of spinnaker nylon or Dacron band along the four edges, then thread a piece of line through the hem of the two shorter edges and attach clips to all four ends. Do not forget to stitch the line onto the hem so that the diaper remains in place! The bridle lines are attached to two of the clips, the control lines to the other two. It is that simple.

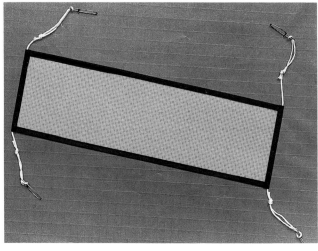

1 The diaper is easy to make: basically a rectangular piece of gauze.

2 The diaper 'in action'.

98

II QUAD-LINE GRIPS

enerally, not only do quad-line grips
come in a fixed size, but you also need
a separate winder to store the lines on.
Our design does not have this disadvantage.

The lower part of our grips has several holes
so that you can adjust the leverage of the grips
according to taste. The leverage of the grips not
only depends on the kind of quad-line kite you
fly but also on the wind conditions under which
you fly. In strong winds you would decrease the
leverage, in light winds increase it. It is merely a
question of placing the end-loop through one of
the holes and placing this around the tip of the
grip. It is better not to use rings, clips and/or
swivels because the upper lines could get caught
in them when making sharp manoeuvres with
the kite.

The integrated winder is part of the lower
lever (where it is not in the way) and its length
makes for quick winding.

MATERIALS
30 x 40 cm board of birch-plywood, 4 mm thick;
20 cm elastic band; 10 cm Velcro; 2 foam rubber
tubes (as used for bicycle handlebars).

PROCEDURE
First make two small templates from a thick
sheet of cardboard according to the figure.
Trace the shape of template A four times onto
the plywood, template B twice. Then saw out
the pieces.

The actual grip is formed by placing the wider
board between the two narrow boards and
gluing them together. For this use waterproof
glue. When the glue has dried completely, file
and sandpaper the grips until the edges are well-
rounded and their surface nice and smooth.

*1 Measurements
of grips.*

*2 The lower control
line is hooked
around the end of
the grip.*

*3 Quad-line grips.
Left: Revolution
grips; right:
Quadriphant grips.*

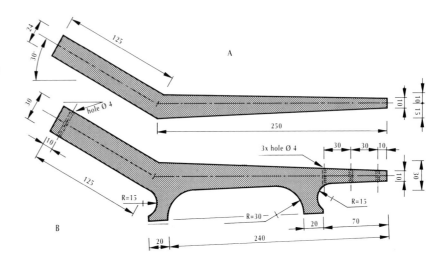

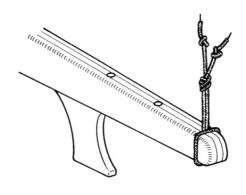

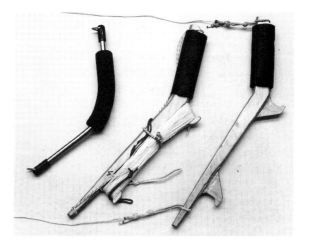

The holes for the lines are not drilled from the side
but from front to back. The upper line is attached
'permanently'. The lower line is connected to a
loop consisting of five separate knots; the length
of the line is adjusted by connecting the line to
one of the knots with a lark's head. The loop is
then pushed through the desired hole and looped
around the tip of the grip.

For a comfortable grip, standard handlebar
padding (from your local bike shop) can be
placed on the wide upper part of the hand grip.

The wrapped up control lines are held in place
by a 10 cm long piece of elastic band with Velcro
sewn onto its edges.

III BUGGY

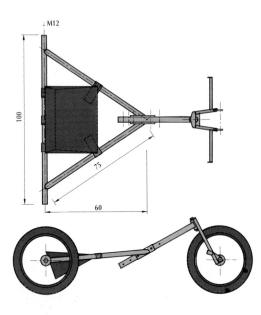

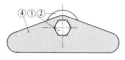

1 *Three-wheel buggy.*

(1) stainless steel bolt M8 x 20 mm
(2) nylon bushing
(3) aluminium Ø 14 x 64 mm
(4) steel strip 4 x 30 mm
(5) front fork tube Ø 16 x 1 x 330 mm
(6) headstem Ø 30 x 1 x 60 mm
(7) stainless steel bolt M12 x 100 mm
(8) steel bushing Ø 15 x 1,5 x 55 mm
(9) steel bushing, M12 thread
(10) sealed ball bearing Ø 28 x 12 x 8 mm
(11) rear axle Ø 30 x 1 x1000 mm
(12) aluminium hub, 28 spoke holes

FRAME MATERIAL:
0,6 m   strip 4 x 30 mm
1,5 m   tube Ø 16 x 1 mm
2,6 m   tube Ø 30 x 1 mm
0,5 m   square tube 30 x 1,5 mm

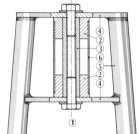

2 *The head set.*

3 *Attachment of one of the rear wheels with sealed ball-bearings.*

Building a buggy involves some skills which most kite flyers and makers may not have. However, these skills are quite easy to attain and if you have a solid bench-vice to clamp steel pipes, a standard hacksaw, a couple of flat and round files and an electric drill you are quite a way towards your goal. To 'bake' the pieces together, you do need welding or soldering equipment. With some luck (and negotiating), however, you may find a friend or colleague who is willing to weld a buggy frame for you at their company's workshop in exchange for a Sputnik. For our soldering work, we use bottles of oxygen and propane gas with an accompanying torch - an investment of about US $150 - US $ 250 (less than an average sewing machine). By using bronze, brass or silver solder, you can easily make steel, stainless steel and brass

pipe joints. We can assure you that working with this sort of hardware is just as easy as working with a sewing machine and it is not difficult to learn.

We have, by the way, come across buggies made out of everything, from steamed beech wood and screw-on aluminum to TIG-welded titanium and glass-fibre/polyester. We understand there is even a carbon-fibre buggy under construction.

DESIGN
Below you will find a list of criteria and requirements that a buggy should meet:
- extremely stable (to prevent toppling over);
- good tracking at high speeds;
- small turning circle;
- comfortable for long distances;
- usable on hard and soft sand, asphalt and grass;
- easy to adjust for different riders
(authors: 1.65 m - 1.90 m);
- easy to disassemble and fold into a compact package;
- easy to build.

It is difficult to combine all these criteria in a single design. We have therefore come up with two entirely different buggy designs whose components are interchangeable: the 'modular system'. With this system, the back part of Buggy #1, for example, can be combined with the front part of Buggy #2, or vice versa. This system can even be extended to constructions for sailing, skiing on snow or skating on ice.

Buggy #1 is a three-wheeler which we have kept as basic as possible. Its frame is made up of only four pipes and a fork from a child's bicycle. This buggy complies with all the above criteria, but after a season of serious buggying your demands will be-

come more complex:
- You prefer better high-speed tracking in order to feel comfortable at 60 km/h and above.
- On reaching courses or tacking into strong winds you want to delay sideways skidding with the front or rear wheels as long as possible and, when the wheels do let go, you want the front and rear wheels to skid simultaneously.
- You want a buggy seat with improved grip in order to prevent being flung out.

Buggy #2 was created as a result of these more specialised demands, resulting in the following modifications:
- the back part of the seat became 'deeper', providing a tighter fit. The location of the rear axle moved further back and became adjustable so that the centre of gravity is now more balanced between front and back wheels.
- two wheels replaced the single wheel in the front; the location of the front axle is also adjustable according to the desired weight distribution and steering characteristics.

The four-wheel buggy does not topple over easily and by varying the lengths of the lever in the indirect joint between the pedals and the front wheels, one can steer the buggy 'aggressively' on short-track races or calmly on long distance and high speed courses. By simply using the improved rear part of Buggy #2 together with the front part of Buggy #1 the desired improvements can be obtained.

MATERIAL
Because buggies are mostly used on beaches, stainless steel is naturally the best material for the frame. But it is a tough material and difficult to work with. You can use plain steel, central heating pipes or even steel pipes from old bicycles, especially if you

have access to simple electrical welding equipment that does not handle stainless steel. But remember, if the beach is your regular buggy terrain you are going to have a constant battle against corrosion.

BRAZING
From the many types of steel available these days, an amateur can make a very respectable looking brazed joint. To connect thin-walled tubes, brazing is even easier than welding. For the sake of clarity, in the case of soldering or brazing, two pieces of metal are joined together by adding another kind of metal with a lower melting point; in our case, brass or bronze. In the case of welding (with a flame or electrically) two pieces of steel are in fact melted together, normally by adding extra steel. Welding is done at a much higher temperature; if you are new to welding you may easily melt a hole in the 1 to 1.5 mm walls of the tubes and ruin the frame. The higher temperatures of welding compared to brazing also affect the strength of the steel around the joint. So, there are some good

reasons to consider brazing even though it is considered an inferior technique by some.

What do you need? A bottle of propane gas with

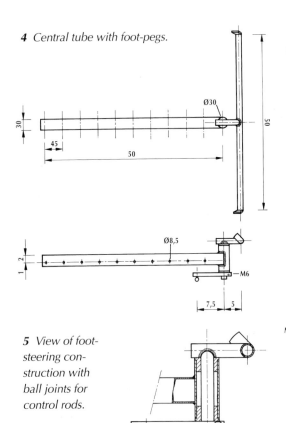

4 Central tube with foot-pegs.

5 View of foot-steering construction with ball joints for control rods.

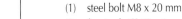

7 The front axle is made out of 40 mm diameter stainless steel tubes.

6 Construction of the front wheel steering system.

a valve, a bottle of oxygen with a pressure reducing valve, accompanying oxygen/propane torch and a pair of not too dark welding goggles. You can also rent this sort of equipment. The solder comes in the form of long round or square rods filled with soldering powder (borax), or as rods coated with this powder. There are various types of soldering alloys with diverse melting-points and viscosity on the market, but you will probably not come across them since the average hardware store only stocks

one or two types. Buy a couple of rods of the various types (they are less than a dollar per piece) and do some experimenting first. Usually a low-viscosity solder works easiest; it flows evenly into the narrow cracks at the rear wheel attachment, for example. The highest viscosity solder actually makes a thicker, and therefore, stronger joint, and easily bridges gaps that may have to be filled due to poor filing and shaping.

Brazing: start with a simple horizontal perpendicular joint between a round and a square tube. It is very important to keep the surface of the metal completely clean and free of grease. Place the two

tubes at the desired position with clamps. Light the torch, first the propane only (yellow flame), then slowly turn on the oxygen until you get a blue flame with a bright blue-white core of about 10 mm. Heat both pipes on the spots you wish to braze; hold the centre of the flame cone 1 - 2 cm from the metal and direct it in such a way that after 10 - 20 seconds both pipes begin to glow red. By placing the solder rod, at that moment, in front of

(1)	steel bolt M8 x 20 mm
(2)	front axle Ø 40 x 1 mm
(3)	tube Ø 25 x 1,5 mm
(4)	nylon bushing
(5)	nut M12
(6)	flattened tube Ø 20 x 1,5 mm
(7)	control lever 4 mm
(8)	top connector 4 mm
(9)	aluminium Ø 14 mm
(10)	steering stop Ø 20 x 1,5 mm

FRAME MATERIAL:

1 m	tube Ø 40 x 1 mm
5 m	tube Ø 25 x 1 mm
1 m	tube Ø 20 x 1 mm
0,5 m	square tube 40 x 1 mm
0,6 m	tube Ø 16 x 1 mm
1 m	strip 40 x 4 mm
2 m	tube Ø 12 x 1 mm

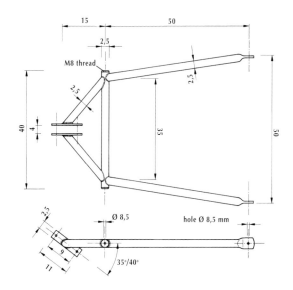

8 *Measurements of the four-wheel buggy parts.*

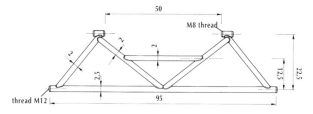

9 *Rear axle and seat-frame.*

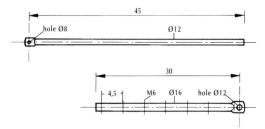

10 *These tubes are shoved into each other, allowing the position of the rear axle to be changed.*

the flame for a short while, the solder will drip onto the corners and then flow out onto both pipes. Then slowly go around the entire joint as the solder drips onto it. If the solder does not flow it means the metal is not clean enough or not hot enough. But do not heat up the metal more than necessary to make the solder flow because overheating causes the soldering-alloy to become brittle.

WHEELS

For practical reasons we have selected wheels in the range of 40 cm diameter because there is a variety of tires available in this size, usually called 16 inch. For example 16" x 2.0 with a simple road profile is more than adequate. In any case, do not use cross-country tires with large knobs. The standard front wheel of a child's bicycle can only be used for the front wheel of a three-wheel buggy. The other wheels are mounted from one side and will have to withstand a lot of sideways force. Special hubs are necessary for this. Wheelchair hubs can also be used but nowadays custom-made wheels for buggies are readily available in many kite shops.

Plastic wheels with fat tires (400 x 100 mm, also referred to as 16 x 4) normally used for wheelbarrows, work well on beaches but should be fitted with sealed ball bearings. With fat tires your speed on hard surfaces may decrease somewhat, but if the beach has

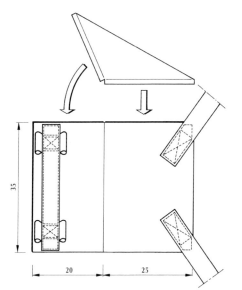

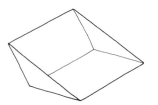

11 *Measurements of the seat. The seat consists of a double layer of canvas. A sheet of triplex is inserted into the back-support. Several holes are made on the bottom of the seat so that water can drain.*

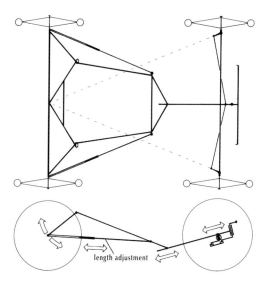

12 *The four-wheel buggy and its adjustable parts.*

14 *The speedometre is placed in a protective frame: frame and speedometer are covered with a silicone coating.*

13 Four-wheel buggy at top speed.

soft sand here and there, your average speed will be higher. Putting fat tires on the rear of the buggy and a standard wheel on the front is a practical compromise.

Buggy tires wear out extremely fast on asphalt and concrete - you can literally follow the rubber tracks they leave behind. In this case it is best to use wheelbarrow wheels with so-called high-speed tires.

SEAT
The seat is sewn out of canvas as per the measurements given. For extra strength and comfort, use double panels and fill them with a layer of foam,

similar to the construction of the harness (see page 105); use 4 - 5 cm wide webbing and sturdy buckles to attach the seat to the frame.

SPEEDOMETER
When you have finally mastered buggy-riding, you may want to know how fast you are travelling. An electronic bicycle speedometer is the best meter for this purpose, but do not be surprised if the results are disappointing; seated so low to the ground on a buggy, you feel like you are going 80 km/h when in reality you are barely hitting the 40 km/h mark. When you go shopping for a speedometer keep the following in mind: it should fit various wheel-sizes (at least 16"), speed readings should include at least

15 A tandem-joint connects two buggies.

80 km/h (the expensive and popular Catseye does not), it should have a programme which can store the maximum speed and should be 100 per cent water-tight. It is also advisable to secure the speedometer into a metal box for protection and to coat it with a layer of silicone; silicone being an elastic material, you will still be able to use the protruding knobs.

IV HARNESS

Flying stunt kites can be physically exhausting. In strong winds the larger Sputnik, for example, can pull so hard that at a certain moment your hands and arms simply give up. By redirecting much of the pull to a harness around your waist, you can persevere much longer in the tug-of-war struggle with your kite.

Hip belts used in mountain climbing and so-called surf-trapezes work well, but you can also make a harness yourself.

A harness consists of a double layer of fabric: a heavy outer layer of corduroy or canvas-like material and a thinner inner layer of approx. 1 oz. spinnaker, for example. A sturdy foam-like material (e.g. used in camping mattresses) fits in-between the two layers of fabric. The camber which appears when the harness is put together is necessary for a proper fit. The shape of the harness should be such that it remains fixed to the buttocks - you should not feel the pull of the kite on the straps between your legs. If necessary adjust the shape of the camber to the shape of your buttocks.

CUTTING

First make two cardboard templates according to the shapes given. Draw the side panel twice and the centre panel once onto the canvas as

MATERIAL	
1 m	heavy duty webbing, 4 - 5 cm wide
2 m	heavy duty webbing, 2 - 3 cm wide
3 pcs	adjustable snaps for the 2 - 3 cm webbing
30 cm	spinnaker nylon, 65 g/m² (1 oz.)
30 cm	canvas or similar material, 200 - 300 g/m²
1 pc	50 x 50 closed cell-foam, 10 mm thick

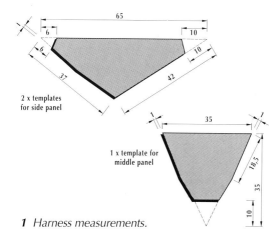

1 Harness measurements.

well as onto the nylon. Canvas should be cut with scissors, but if you are using corduroy or some synthetic material it is better to hot-cut. To prevent fraying, it is advisable to hot-cut the straps to size with a hot-cutter.

The foam is also marked with the help of the template, but it needs to be cut approximately 15 mm smaller than the template measurements, otherwise it does not fit.

STITCHWORK

Sew the seams by placing the various pieces on top of each other. Stitch 1 cm from the edge; the loose ends will later be folded inside.

First sew the three canvas pieces together with a 1 cm wide seam. At this point try on the harness and adjust it to the shape of your buttocks.

Now sew the webbing onto the right side of the canvas - first the two main straps of 3-4 cm webbing onto the left and right side; the shorter two narrow straps (including the snaps) are then stitched at an angle on top of the wider ones. The long straps that will run between the legs are sewn

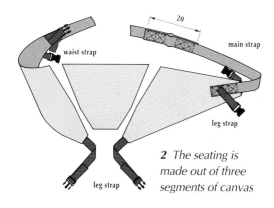

2 The seating is made out of three segments of canvas

onto the centre canvas panel.

Sew the spinnaker pieces together. The entire piece is then placed on top of the canvas with the right sides of the nylon and canvas together. Make a 1 cm seam all the way round, with all the straps facing inside of course. Leave the wide side on top of the central parts open (the foam is later inserted here). While sewing the tips on the left and right, the straps tightening the harness around your waist are placed between the two layers of fabric and stitched along. Now turn the whole thing inside out - the webbings will appear on the proper side. It is time to try it on now. If everything is alright get on with the foam; press the two side pieces in their respective places and close them by stitching on top of the existing stitches. Push the foam into the centre panel and stitch the last seam, folding the remaining 1 cm edge inside.

All you have to do now is join the two wide main straps together, overlapping them by 20 cm. A 2.5 cm gap will remain in the middle where you can attach a carbine hook or a safety release for connection to your steering system. Attach adjustable snaps onto both leg and waist straps.

Now you should be able to fly your favorite power-kite for hours on end!

V POWER STEERING

A harness is not enough. There has to be a connection between the control lines and the harness: i.e. power steering.

The heart of the matter with power steering lies in a reliable and smooth running pulley system, preferably one with ball bearings. Most shops selling water sports goods have a wide selection of such pulley systems including 5 - 6 mm Ø braided polyester lines.

The pulley is attached to the harness by means of a quick-release device. Thanks to this shackle you can disconnect the kite from the harness very quickly. Keep in mind, however, that this method is not very 'safe'. In emergencies you hardly have time to look for this 'safety-release', as it is sometimes called. We use the harness for power steering only for long distances, not for flying larger kites than we are normally capable of controlling. In fact, whenever we are in doubt whether we can control a kite in certain wind conditions or not, we first fly the kite without a harness for a while until we are certain of being capable of controlling it sufficiently.

PROCEDURE

First thread the line through the pulley and make two overhand securing knots at the ends. Then place the line in the zigzag form as shown in the figure. There should be a 25 cm difference between the securing knots and the pulley.

The control line attachments can now be secured with overhand knots or, even better, with a zigzag stitch.

```
MATERIALS
 4 m    braided polyester line, 5-6 mm thick
 1 pc   pulley of at least ←//→ 300 kg
 3 pcs  carbine hooks
 1 pc   stainless steel quick-release shackle
```

The 25 cm difference mentioned above determines the distance between your body and your hands but depends, of course, on the grips you use as well as on the actual distance between the pulley and your body. If necessary, adjust the 25 cm so that only your elbows remain bent when flying the kite in a straight line.

The carbine hooks are for the attachments to the control lines and for the connections to the harness.

You can use Skyclaws or padded straps, connected to the securing knots with lark's heads.

CONTROL-ROPE

While buggying for long distances you often have to keep your hands in a fixed position. For example, if your kite is flying towards the left, you have to keep your right hand closer to your body to prevent the kite from crashing to the ground. This uneven position can become quite tiring, even when wearing a harness. To solve the problem replace your hand grips with a 'control-rope', a loop-shaped 2 cm thick braided or twisted nautical line with five knots - 15 cm apart - on both ends. Because the pulley absorbs most of the power, the grip on these knots is sufficient for controlling the kite. What you actually have are five grips on both ends of the loop from which you can always choose the most comfortable position. While on a long-distance reach you can even let go of one hand.

On light wind days, when you are buggying with very large kites, the control input with your arms can sometimes be too little to make certain kites turn. Take for example a 10 m² Sputnik or a stack of 10 ft Flexifoils. The control-rope, however, serves as an extension of your arms, because you can take the line in on one side by using both hands if necessary. This makes it possible to manoeuvre the 10 m² Sputnik in tight loops even in 3 Beaufort winds.

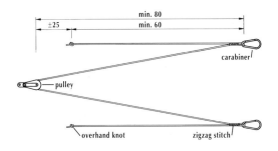

1 Zigzag line of power-steering.
On the two ends grips or wrist-straps are attached.

2 Harness with grip line.

3 Grip line.

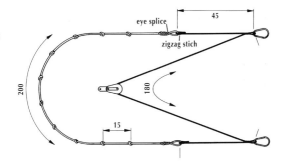

VI STACKING KITES

The stacking of kites causes traction to increase. A stack of kites is also attractive to look at.

The increase of traction is almost in proportion to the number of stacked kites, though the pull of three single kites is slightly stronger than that of three kites stacked in a train. The positive thing about stacking kites is that you can select the exact pull you want by the number of kites you stack.

But stacking also has disadvantages. Launching the kites can be disastrous - some bad luck and the kites fly out of control and become hopelessly tangled; you then find yourself spending the rest of the afternoon trying to undo the mess. Kite stacks also take up a lot of space, they do not attain the speeds that single kites do, and react rather slowly to commands. Furthermore, the Law of Murphy is certainly applicable: everything that can go wrong does go wrong. Just when you have finally launched the stack after ten frustrating attempts, one of the spreaders will come loose.

Kites such as the Spin-off are stacked on five lines. Take five lines of the same length, approximately the length of the leading edges. With a lark's head, attach them to the front of the add-on or stacker kite. Make five loop knots approximately 15 cm long. Then with a lark's head attach these to the reverse side of the first kite. Remember that the loop around the cross-joint will be shorter because the cross-joint is thicker than the leading edges (to which the other five lines are attached). Make sure this loop is longer. Now with a lark's head tie the loops of the first kite to the lines of the second kite.

It is not necessary to take off the bridles of the add-on kites, but it does look better and it reduces some of the chaos if mishaps occur.

In a large train of kites, the spars of the first kites can become crushed where the kites are connected; the lines are, after all, attached around the carbon tubes. In this case it is best to connect the five loops to the stack lines rather than to the frame (and in the case of the first kite of the train to the kite's bridle). The train now pulls at the lines, not at the frames.

The longer the stack of kites, the stronger the breaking strength of the line should be. Because the kites at the front of the stack must withstand most of the pull, their lines have to be the thickest.

Flyers who fly stacks regularly usually work with 'stack sections'. These are ready-made sets of, for example, three add-on kites. The set with the thinnest lines goes to the rear, those with the thickest to the front. Therefore, adding or taking off kites is done right behind the first kite (the only one with a bridle) and not at the end of the train.

In a large train, the first kite will be exposed to the highest forces and should be completely reinforced (thicker tubes for the frame, more spreaders, wider Dacron sleeves and more reinforcement pieces): use long, thick bridle lines and buy the best clips available.

A Speedwing needs three lines for stacking but otherwise it works as the above. We prefer using a 2 - 3 cm longer nose-line on the last Speedwing. This makes the kite fly at a steeper angle, pulling the whole train tighter.

A stack of Neptunes, *kites by Joel Scholz.*

Seven lines are attached to the quad-line Revolution. Take off the bridle of the add-on kite and attach the stack lines to the same points (wing tips, in the middle, and two on each spine).

Similar to this method, a Kwat would need stack lines on eleven points. Alas, we have not yet given this one a try.

Sputniks and Peels can also be stacked. However, we are not enthusiastic about the idea (hard to launch, risk of total chaos, etc.) so we have not spent much time experimenting with it. We prefer controlling the traction by varying the size of a Sputnik rather than increasing the number of kites.

VII KNOTS

Half-hitch knot. This knot prevents the ends of lines from fraying; but more importantly, the half-hitch knot prevents knots such as the bridle knot from coming loose.

Overhand knot. Just a half-hitch in a doubled-over line - the simplest way to make loops on bridle lines.

Lark's Head. We use this knot often because not only is it reliable but it is also easy to untie. This knot is used, for example, to connect bridle lines to a kite frame or to connect lines to loops.

Bridle knot. This knot connects primary bridle lines of a sparless kite to its ribs. The same knot is also used to connect lines to rings or clips. The advantage of this knot, compared to other knots, is that the length of the line is always exactly the same. This knot will keep a bridle completely symmetrical.

In the construction plans of Sputnik 4 you can read about how this knot is used on sparless kites. Attaching this knot to a ring works as follows: make a securing knot at the end of the line. Push the line through the ring and wrap the loose end twice around the fixed end. Now push the loose end through the first loop of the wound line. Pull on the knot until the securing knot is flush against the wound line.

Sheet Bend. This knot comes in two forms: single and double. The double sheet bend is more reliable, but the single one is also very satisfactory. We use the sheet bend to connect secondary bridle lines to primary bridle lines. The single sheet bend is easier to untie and therefore more appropriate for bridle lines; adjustments are made faster and more accurately.

Sleeves. Knots in Dyneema and Spectra flying lines should be made with a sleeve covering the line at the place where the knots are made. In order to make a protective sleeve you need a thick braided line of approx. 30 cm length. Remove the core (a fluffy strand of threads) from the line with your nails. Pull the control line through the sleeve by means of a thin doubled-up piano wire. Tie an ordinary overhand knot at the end. Use it once to fly your kite. The lines will no doubt stretch unequally. Shorten the longest line, check once again if both lines are of equal lengths now. If so, tie a second overhand knot in the loop, so as to prevent the control line from slipping inside the sleeve.

Repairs. There is but one solution for broken Dyneema or Spectra: braiding. Use a blunt darning needle (or a doubled-up piano wire) to braid one of the ends three times through the other line, starting at 10 cm from the rupture-point. With the darning needle work the end away into the core of the line. Repeat the procedure with the other end. This method is even stronger than a sleeve-and-knot, providing an entirely smooth connection.

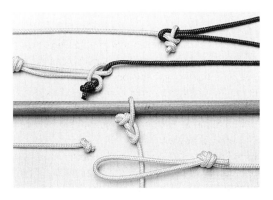

1 Knots used in this book. From top to bottom: single sheet bend with securing knot, lark's head on line with securing knot, bridle knot (around tube), line with securing knot (left) and loop with overhand knot.

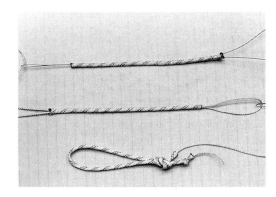

2 Lines with Kevlar and Dyneema require sleeves at the ends. From top to bottom: piano wire through sleeve, control line pulled through sleeve, overhand knot for the loop.

VIII COMPUTER PROGRAMME

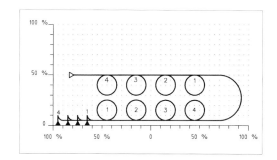

For the very demanding kite flyer and designer, there is a floppy disk with two computer programmes which can be purchased along with this book. The first programme, *KiteFlight*, shows complete S.T.A.C.K. compulsory figures 'live' on the computer screen. With a minimal amount of programming, you can add your own figures to this programme as well. The other programme, *The Plotter*, combines an ingenious calculating programme with a plotting function. It allows you to alter and recalculate the measurements and bridle configurations of the sparless kites presented in this book. The plotting sub-routine enables most computer printers to print out templates for several kites in this book in accordance with their true sizes.

The disk is purchased separate from the book. This was done deliberately so that readers un- interested in computers would not feel compelled to purchase the programme.

We would like to stress that *Stunt Kites II* is self-supporting, so that the disk is in no way necessary for understanding the book. Construction plans for each kite are fully explained and all measurements clearly given. The disk is purely for kite builders who want to modify kite models presented in the book and for flyers who are seriously considering competition-flying.

Contact your local kite store if you are interested in purchasing the above disk.

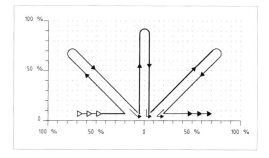

A few figures from S.T.A.C.K.'s book.
Top: 'large hairpin and landing',
bottom: 'starburst and return'.

S.T.A.C.K.

Sport Team and Competitive Kiting, or S.T.A.C.K., is an international association which takes stunt kite flying very seriously. S.T.A.C.K. organises competitions both regionally and nationally all over the world, which eventually lead to the annual World Cup Stunt Kite Competition, held at a different venue each time.

S.T.A.C.K. competitions consist of sections for compulsory figures (mostly three), free-style and ballet. During free-style flying, participants show how well they have mastered their kites - this section is performed without music. The objective of the ballet section - which is performed to music - is to convey human emotions through the movements of the kites. With their kites, participants try to impress the public with astonishing manoeuvres, creative compositions and surprising launching and landing techniques.

The winners of each competition are chosen by a jury, its members obviously wielding quite some power. This has recently led to an on-going discussion about the quality of judging, especially in the US where attractive sponsor contracts are involved.

S.T.A.C.K. does train jury members and publishes a booklet explaining what jury members should look for when judging, but this will not solve all the problems. Subjectivity, for example, seems inevitable because it is almost impossible to appraise beauty and originality for their 'true' value.

The compulsory figures to be performed at a competition are announced by the jury or organisers a few weeks prior to the event. Each competition has different compulsory figures, all listed in a book published by S.T.A.C.K.

Information regarding S.T.A.C.K. membership and competitions can be found in most kite magazines.

IX READING LIST

S everal new books on stunt kites have appeared in the past few years, most of them originating from Germany. *Drachenmagazin*, also published in Germany, is probably the most interesting magazine for stunt kite flyers.

The only English magazine totally devoted to stunt kites, *Stunt Kite Quarterly* from the US, unfortunately folded in 1993. Of the remaining two kite magazines published in the US - *Kite Lines* and *American Kite* - the latter focuses more on stunt kites than the former one.

To understand the 'peripheral phenomena' of stunt kite flying, the reader must search for information beyond the world of kite flying. There are literally hundreds of books on aerodynamics, sailing and hydrofoils; below, under the heading BUGGIES, BOATS AND HYDROFOILS, you will find a list of books we used as reference material.

BOOKS

Stunt kites

- Erfurth, Thomas & Schlitzer, Harald, *Lenkdrachen zum Nachbauen*, Englisch Verlag, 1989 (German)
- Gomberg, David, *Stuntkites!*, David Gomberg, Salem, 1988 (English)
- Van der Horst, Servaas and Velthuizen, Nop, *Stunt Kites - To Make and Fly*, Thoth Publishers, Bussum, 1991 (Dutch and English)
- Moulton, Ron, *Kites, a Practical Handbook for the Modern Kite Flyer*, Argus Books, Hemel & Hempstead, 1992 (English)
- Reich, Ron, *Kite Precision - Your Comprehensive Guide for Flying Controllable Kites*, Tutor Text, Ramona, 1993 (English)
- Rieleit, Peter, *Leistungsstarke Lenkdrachen zum Nachbauen*, Ravensburger Buchverlag, 1993 (German)
- Rocker, H.E., *Lenkdrachen-ABC*, Drachenverlag, Hamburg, 1992 (German)
- Schertel, Christine, *Skywork Experience*, Skywork Agentur, Hamburg, 1991 (German)
- Schertel, Christine, *Skywork Experience II*, Skywork Agentur, Hamburg, 1993 (German)
- Schimmelpfennig, Wolfgang, *Lenkdrachen, Bauen und Fliegen*, Falken-Verlag, Niedernhausen/Ts, 1989 (German)
- Schimmelpfennig, Wolfgang, *Phantastische Drachenwelt*, Falken-Verlag, Niedernhausen/Ts, 1991 (German)
- Schimmelpfennig, Wolfgang, *Neue Lenkdrachen und Einleiner*, Falken-Verlag, Niedernhausen/Ts, 1993 (German)
- Synergy, Richard, *Stunt Kite Basics*, Fly Write Publications, 1993 (English)

Buggies, boats and hydrofoils

- Baader, Juan, *Zeilsport, Zeiltechniek, Zeiljachten*, Hollandia Inc., Baarn, 1976 (Dutch)
- Grogono, James, *Icarus, the Boat that Flies*, Adlard Coles Nautical, London, 1987 (English)
- Lynn, Peter, *Buggies, Boats & Peels*, Aeolus Press, Randallstown, 1992 (English)
- Marchaj, C.A., *Aero-hydrodynamics of Sailing*, Adlard Coles Nautical, London, 1988 (English)

MAGAZINES

- *American Kite*, Daniel Prentice, San Francisco, as from 1988 (English)
- *Drachenmagazine*, Axel Voss, Drachen Verlag, Hamburg, as from 1989 (German)
- *Kite Lines*, Aeolus Press, Randallstown, as from 1977 (English)
- *Sport & Design Drachen*, Verlag für Technik und Handwerk, Baden-Baden, as from 1993 (German)
- *Vlieger*, Stichting Nederlandse Vliegerpromotie, The Hague, as from 1982 (Dutch)

INTERNET

Stunt kite fanatics can obtain up-to-date information through electronic mail. The newsgroup for kiteflyers with access to Internet is called: rec.kites.

X CONVERSIONS

We strongly advize you to use as little conversion as possible. The kites in this book are based on the metric system; by converting measurements of the various plans into feet and inches you are likely to get 'odd' numbers. That is to say, converting the measurements, you will end up rounding off whereby precision will be lost. Why not buy yourself some metric rulers instead? It would be worth the investment.

WIND SPEED SCALE

Beaufort	m/s	km/h	mph	knots
1	0-2	0-7	0-4	0-4
2	2-3	7-11	4-7	4-6
3	3-5	11-20	7-13	6-11
4	5-8	20-28	13-18	11-16
5	8-11	28-38	18-24	16-21
6	11-14	38-50	24-31	21-28
7	14-17	50-61	31-38	28-34
8	17-20	61-72	38-45	34-40
9	20-24	72-86	45-54	40-48

LENGTH

1 m	= 3.28 feet
1 cm	= 0.394 inch
1 mm	= 0.039 inch

WEIGHT

1 kg	= 2.205 lb
1 gram	= 0.035 oz

SPEED

1 km/h	= 0.62 mph

MOST COMMON METRIC MATERIALS — - IMPERIAL ALTERNATIVES

MOST COMMON METRIC MATERIALS	- IMPERIAL ALTERNATIVES
Ripstop nylon, 30-40 gram	- 0.75 oz
Solid fibreglass rod 3-4 mm	- 1/8" glassfibre rod
Solid carbon fibre rod 2-3 mm	- 3/32" carbon rod, or 1/8" glassfibre
Carbon fibre tube 6 mm	- 0.22 inches lighter alternative
	- 1/4" heavier alternative
Carbon fibre tube 8 mm	- 0.35-0.414 inch epoxy tube

COMMON LINE BREAKING-STRENGTH

35 kg	- 80 lb	small kites/light wind kites
65 kg	- 150 lb	medium kites/team flying
90 kg	- 200 lb	large kites/strong wind team flying
135 kg	- 300 lb	power kites
225 kg	- 500 lb	traction kites

S*tunt Kites To Make and Fly* is meant for two categories of stunt kite flyers: for those who have bought a kite and now want to run the thing for all it is worth and for the stunt flyer who wants to build his own kites.

The book covers every aspect of stunt flying ranging from stunt kite history, control lines and knots to suitable flying grounds. It informs the novice kite flyer about the various existing stunt kites, power-kiting, precision flying, quad-line flying and even team formation flying. The second part of *Stunt Kites* contains detailed construction specifications for eleven different kite models, from the very simple to the extremely complicated design. It's a great help for making the right choice of material too.

WARNING! After reading this book you may become a stunt kite addict... just like the rest of us.

Paperback, 26 x 21 cm (landscape)
96 pages with 150 photographs and drawings
(black-and-white and color)
ISBN 90 6868 052 8
Published by: THOTH Publishers,
Bussum, the Netherlands

STUNT KITES
TO MAKE AND FLY

Servaas van der Horst
Nop Velthuizen

THE PRESS ABOUT *STUNT KITES TO MAKE AND FLY*:

'In a world full of stunter-hunger, stunt kite books are still playing catch-up. Here's one that helps. (...) *Stunt Kites* is appealing: well laid out with quality photographs and drawings. Color photos in judicious quantity do a great deal to appetize.'
— Valerie Govig in *Kite Lines*

'(...) this is the definitive handbook on sport kiting. Written with clarity and humor and translated smoothly into English, the book is a professional production throughout, as engaging for the expert as it is instructional for the beginner.'
— Daniel Prentice in *American Kite*